OPERATION ANTHROPOID

Reinhard Heydrich:
ASSASSINATION!

Ray R. Cowdery
with
Peter Vodenka

Library of Congress Cataloging in Publication Data

USM, Incorporated
International Standard Book Number (ISBN) 0-910667-42-X (softcover only)

    Cowdery, Ray R.   1941-
    with Vodenka, Peter   1955-
Title: **REINHARD HEYDRICH: ASSASSINATION!**
    First American Edition

1. *Biography* - Heydrich, Reinhard 1904-1942; National Socialists; SS
2. *History* - World War II; National Socialists; Underground Movements - Czechoslovakia; SS; Lidice

Printed in the United States of America

                              Copyright © 1994 by
                               Ray R. Cowdery
                               All Rights Reserved
                               First American Edition
                                    98765432

WARNING
This book is protected by international copyright. No part of it may be reproduced
by electronic, mechanical, or other means (except for critical reviews)
without the prior written permission of the distributor. Any and all violations
of this copyright will be prosecuted to the full extent of the law.

VAROVÁNÍ
Tato kniha je pod ochranou zákona o mezinárodním autorském právu. Kniha sama a ůžádná
jeji část nesmí být žádným způsobem bez povolení vydavatele kopírována. Jakékoli porušení
tohoto žákona budie trestáno v plném rozsahu.

DISTRIBUTED EXCLUSIVELY
WORLDWIDE BY

USM, Incorporated
Post Office Box 810
Lakeville, MN 55044-0810 USA
Fax (612) 469-4928

Reinhard Heydrich: Assassination

INTRODUCTION

This book is the result of a combination of great interest, persistence and good luck. When I began the project I planned to produce a small book of the type so popular today - lots of photos and captions and no text at all. The more research I did the more obvious it became that there was a dearth of objective literature on the subject. The principal literature on Reinhard Heydrich relies heavily on the outrageously biased and manipulated "research" of Shlomo Aronson and much of the rest is yellow-page journalism. While there is not the slightest doubt about the extreme courage and self-sacrifice of Josef Gabčík and Jan Kubiš, some of that which has been written in early books about the Czechoslovakian parachutists sent to kill Heydrich finds its source in extremely heroic nationalistic propaganda* produced during World War II to make the Allies feel better about their undercover efforts. During the decades of communist rule in Czechoslovakia after World War II all information concerning the training of Czechoslovakian parachutists and their subsequent effort to kill Reinhard Heydrich was twisted and changed for communist purposes. The communists had no use for heroes that had been trained, led and maneuvered from Britain. I decided there should be a decent book covering this important piece of history and I have tried to write it.

What happened at Lidice, Czechoslovakia in the Summer of 1942 is among my earliest childhood memories. In my small town in Minnesota people spoke of what happened in Lidice as if it had happened 40 or 50 miles away. As a boy I was always horrified by reports of the killing and destruction in Lidice and determined to visit the place someday.

I went to the country that was formerly Czechoslovakia (now the Czech Republic and Slovakia) many times during the bad old days of the communist regime to complete research for books I was then writing about the American military jeeps of World War II. Many of the rarest of those jeeps were given to the government of Czechoslovakia after the war and are still there today. With the greatest difficulties I also visited all the historic places I could find which were connected to the Czechoslovakian resistance, the death of Reinhard Heydrich and the destruction of Lidice during World War II. They were very difficult to find. The direct response to inquiries was most often, "You can not go there", or "The weekly bus just left", or "That place no longer exists". Harassment was common when a foreigner exhibited an interest in the subject. I reached Lidice the first time by asking directions of everyone I met along the road. Some people within 10 miles of the place claimed to have no idea where it was. There were no road signs pointing the way to Lidice prior to 1989. The rest of the story of this book consists of much better luck.

In 1986 I met Peter Vodenka who had defected from Czechoslovakia with his wife Lilly and their two children in 1983. Peter and I share an interest in old American jeeps and in the wartime history of Czechoslovakia. He knew Jaroslav Čvančara who had written a book in Czech which concentrated heavily on the many Czechoslovakians who had conspired against the German occupation and Heydrich. Peter showed me the Čvančara book and rekindled my interest in Reinhard Heydrich and the Czechoslovakian parachutists sent from England in December 1941 to kill him.

Through Peter Vodenka I met his brother Stanley Vodenka of Mníšek pod Brdy outside Praha, and Jaroslav Čvančara of Praha; two more soul mates for my interest in Czechoslovakian commandos, Reinhard Heydrich, Lidice, etc. Mr Čvančara, son of a theater owner put out of business by the communists, had amassed an amazing archive of material concerning the events of the attempted assassination of Reinhard Heydrich and its aftermath. His interest, knowledge and determination to see history documented correctly led Mr Čvančara to write and publish extensively in Czech on the subject after freedom was restored in Czechoslovakia in 1989. I have drawn heavily on the Čvančara Archive to illustrate this book, and my collaborator Peter Vodenka is responsible for translating the captions Mr Čvančara had written for the photos of the Czechoslovakian parachutists. I accept full responsibility for the information concerning the background of Reinhard Heydrich, the history of Czechoslovakia and the text of this book.

---

*A quotation from the January 1994 issue of US Naval Proceedings sheds light on the use of such propaganda: "Traditions, myths and legends need to be viewed through tinted lenses. They may not be exact prescriptions for today, but they are powerful motivators for which people fight and die".

I have attempted to write this book without bias as I have none. That is a difficult goal when dealing with World War II subjects. Other than Mr Čvančara's work and the book by Edouard Calic, most other sources consulted were heavily biased with unsubstantiated pseudo-historical garbage regarding "Reinhard Heydrich's homosexuality" and, "Reinhard Heydrich's Jewish ancestors", etc. These fabrications are now known to have been the work of the war-time rumor factory of the British War Cabinet's *Joint Intelligence Sub-Committee.* I have been able to find *no* neutral corroboration for fabricated stories such as these.

I would never argue that Heydrich was not brutal in carrying out his responsibilities - he was. And the horrible terror, torture and death that followed in Czechoslovakia in the wake of his death was certainly an outrage with few parallels in history. On the other hand, I served in the US Marine Corps and while serving had an absolute obligation to the oath I had taken to carry out the orders of my superiors without questioning them. Heydrich had much the same responsibility to his superiors and he expected and got immediate obedience from those to whom he gave orders. He was not a participant in an egalitarian situation. Unfortunately, people without military experience have great difficulty understanding that these principles are basic to *all effective* military command structures. Thus, the unfamiliar often attribute standard (if brutal) military behavior to some sort of insanity or perversion. Nothing in my research on either side of the Atlantic causes me to conclude that Heydrich was the least bit insane or perverse.

This is not Reinhard Heydrich's story, but he is central to it. This book is the story of a remarkable soldier, the assassination planned for him by the British Government and/or the Czechoslovakian government-in-exile in Britain, and the aftermath of his death in and around Praha. You will find out who Reinhard Heydrich was, who the heroic Czechoslovakian parachutists were, and why so many died in the wake of the events of "OPERATION ANTHROPOID".

It has always been an irritation to me that I was not taught in school to pronounce the names of places outside of America as the people who live there pronounce them. Rather, I was taught British-English pronunciation. Many years ago on my first visit to Paris, I inquired for directions to the city of Reims (I pronounced it *Reems* as I had been taught) and was unable to make anyone understand me. In this book place names, titles and surnames are generally written in Czech or German rather than English, and a guide to the pronunciation of many may be found in appendix A. This should greatly assist readers that wish to visit the places mentioned, and will make it easier for them to discuss the history of the subject with other interested people.

I wish to thank my wife Josephine for her patience and prodding with reference to this book, and Dr Gaylon Crawford, Dennis Falaas, Margaret van Nierop and Tim Pahl for their assistance with research documentation.

Cowdey

Ray Cowdery
Lakeville, MN
1994

The design depicted above is the composite of a World War II era Czechoslovakian parachutists device ("jump wings") with an Orthodox cross superposed upon the parachute. The composite is intended as a tribute to the Czechoslovakian parachutists who took refuge in the crypt of the Orthodox Cathedral of Saints Cyril and Methodius in Praha and to the clerics who tried to protect them, and gave their lives in the cause of liberation. *This badge is a trademark of USM, Inc. Box 810, Lakeville, MN 55044 USA and may be used by others ONLY with written permission from USM, Inc.*

Josef GABČÍK   Jan KUBIŠ

DEDICATION

This book is dedicated to the memory of Josef Gabčík and Jan Kubiš, two of the men who on 27 May 1942 and against all odds, put their lives on the line in a face-to-face confrontation with Adolf Hitler's personal representative in Czechoslovakia -
SS-Obergruppenführer and Reichsprotektor of Bohemia & Moravia, Reinhard Heydrich.

The wounds they inflicted on Heydrich that morning eventually killed him, setting off the largest manhunt of World War II. For weeks the heroic Czechoslovakian underground was able to hide and protect Gabčík, Kubiš and many of their colleagues. In the end it was not a superior force that ferreted out these commandos, but treachery from within their own ranks. They were betrayed by one of their own.

GABČÍK, KUBIŠ AND THE CZECHOSLOVAKIAN VOLUNTEERS

Josef Gabčík was born 08 April 1912 in Poluvice at Žilina in Slovakia. He learned lock smithing in Bohemia and became a gymnast at Žilina. After military service from 1932-1938 he worked in a military chemical factory. When the German occupation began in March 1939 he resisted at once by refusing to turn over keys and drawings. On 05 May he went underground and crossed the border into Poland.

Jan Kubiš was born 24 June 1913 in Dolní Vilémovice at Třebíče in Moravia. He worked in agriculture and was a member of one of the physical culture organizations, *Orel* (Eagle)*. Kubiš joined the Army in 1935 and served with the 3rd Guard Battalion at Opava during mobilization. Later, he worked in a brick factory. In June 1939 he armed himself with a grenade and crossed into Poland where he joined a Czechoslovakian unit being formed in Krakow.

Both Kubiš and Gabčík served alongside a great many other Czechoslovakian volunteers in the defense of France during the German invasion in May of 1940. Both were decorated for their service during the Battle of the Marne northeast of Paris. With the military collapse of France in a period of just a few days, the Czechoslovakians were moved to the south to prevent their capture. In an unbelievable act of ingratitude the French government disarmed the Czechoslovakian volunteers and turned their confiscated weapons over to the Germans! From southern France the Czechoslovakian troops made their way to England to fight another day.

CZECHOSLOVAKIA

Prior to World War II, Czechoslovakia was an independent country about the size of the American state of New York with a population of around 15-1/2 million. It occupied the very heart of Europe and was the realization of a centuries-old dream to re-establish a country based on the ancient Kingdom of Bohemia. The defeat of Germany and the dismemberment of the Austro-Hungarian Empire at the end of World War I allowed the victors to assemble a new country by combining Austrian *Bohemia and Moravia* with part of German *Silesia,* with heavily Hungarian *Slovakia* and *Ruthenia* (also known then as *Sub-Carpathian Russia*). The new country of Czechoslovakia came into existence on 28 October 1918.

Two ancient mountain systems divided Czechoslovakia from its neighbors: the *Carpathian* in the east and the *Sudeten* along the western border with Germany. The western part of the country was the source of three of Europe's great rivers, the *Odra* (Oder in German) the *Vltava* (Moldau in German) and the *Labe* (Elbe in German). Since Czechoslovakia had no natural outlet to the sea, the peace treaty at the end of World War I gave the new country rights to wharves in the German port cities of Hamburg and Stettin, about 200 miles away.

Czechoslovakia was very rich in natural and human resources, industry and geological beauty. Its farms produced an abundance of animals, fowl, grain, fruit, sugar beets, potatoes, corn and hops. Beer, weapons, munitions and a wide variety of industrial products were exported around the world. Czechoslovakian mines provided great quantities of coal, iron, copper, lead, graphite, garnets and salt.

Small wonder then that German Chancellor Adolf Hitler put Czechoslovakia *second only to his homeland of Austria* on a list of desirable real estate as he planned his "Germanization" of central Europe. The *London Times* newspaper in its 07 September 1938 edition, advocated the annexation to Germany of all German-speaking areas in Czechoslovakia. On 12 September 1938 Hitler demanded that the government of Czechoslovakia return to Germany the 110 square mile *Hlucin* area which the Germans had been required to give up in 1918. On 10 October the German army occupied all of Hlucin and then some. At the subsequent *"Four-Power Conference"* in München (Munich), the ministers of the governments of England, France and Italy agreed with Hitler to one of the great crimes of the century: *that Germany should keep all of the Czechoslovakian territory that its forces had already occupied* (11,701 square miles). In their eagerness to pillage a defenseless nation the *"Four Powers"* also agreed that 4,566 square miles of Czechoslovakia would be ceded to Hungary and 419 square miles of Czechoslovakia (Teschen) would be ceded to Poland! The borders were agreed to by the *"Four Powers"* on 20 November 1938 without asking anyone in or from

---

*Sister organization of the much larger and better known *Sokol* (Falcon).

Czechoslovakia. The lands Czechoslovakia gave up included over 4,900,000 of its people and uncountable resources and industries.

Recognizing that the governments of France and England were paralyzed with fear of confronting him and *would not honor their treaties* to defend what remained of Czechoslovakia, Hitler ordered German forces to occupy all of Bohemia and Moravia on 14 March 1939. The only unoccupied province of Czechoslovakia, Slovakia, declared its independence and signed a 25 year protective treaty with Hitler's Germany. Czechoslovakia, to use Adolf Hitler's words, "ceased to exist" only 20 years after it originally came into being.

Bohemia and Moravia were reorganized as a *Protektorate of the Großdeutsches Reich* (Greater German Reich) and career diplomat Baron Konstantin Freiherr von Neurath was installed as *Reichsprotektor*. Von Neurath was chosen by Hitler because he was an old Weimar diplomat, and not considered by foreign governments to be a Nazi. Parliament was closed, many newspapers and universities were shut down, automobile traffic was shifted from driving on the left to driving on the right, and German law replaced Czech law throughout the Protektorate. The country was run by a National Council subservient to German occupation forces. A Czechoslovakian government-in-exile was formed in London by Dr Eduard Beneš and other expatriates.

The independence movement prior to World War I that resulted in the creation of Czechoslovakia was influenced greatly by Tomáš Masaryk, professor of philosophy at the University of Praha. Among his students were Eduard Beneš and František Moravec, two men who were destined to play major roles in the future governments of Czechoslovakia.

Beneš had fled Austro-Hungarian Praha in 1915, escaping to France where he effectively lobbied the Allies in favor of Czechoslovakian independence. After the creation of Czechoslovakia he served as Foreign Minister until 1935 when President Masaryk fell ill and Beneš succeeded him.

CZECHOSLOVAKIA IN TRANSITION

= 1938 CZECHOSLOVAKIAN BORDER
= INTERNATIONAL BOUNDARIES
= LAND CEDED TO GERMANY 20 NOVEMBER 1938
= LAND CEDED TO HUNGARY 20 NOVEMBER 1938
= LAND CEDED TO POLAND 20 NOVEMBER 1938

GERMAN FORCES SEIZED BOHEMIA AND MORAVIA ON 15 MARCH 1939. SLOVAKIA DECLARED ITS INDEPENDENCE AND RUTHENIA WAS GIVEN TO HUNGARY ON 14 MARCH 1939.

© Copyright 1993 by Ray R. Cowdery

With a full understanding of the fragility of the new composite country of Czechoslovakia, Beneš knew that he could strengthen his position among his foreign supporters by brokering the intelligence data that was changing hands in Praha.

Beneš' chief of military intelligence was another former Masaryk student, Col František Moravec. During World War I Moravec had also fled Praha, deserting the Austro-Hungarian Army and fighting with the Russians against the Bolsheviks in the *Czech Legion*. Together, Beneš and Moravec realized that their access to intelligence information on Hitler's Germany made them very valuable to the intelligence services in Moscow, London and Paris. Beneš sincerely reasoned that if the Soviet Union, England and France were dependent on Czechoslovakia for high grade military intelligence on Germany, they would be likely to defend Czechoslovakia against potential German aggression. As German talk of annexing the Sudetenland escalated, Moravec and Beneš did their best to increase their cooperation with British, French and Soviet intelligence agencies.

The Czechs tried to help by providing aid in the transit of Soviet soldiers on their way to fight in the Spanish civil war. The British Secret Intelligence Service (SIS or MI6) office in Praha soon found they were getting far better military intelligence data on Germany from Moravec for nothing than their own agents were able to obtain at great cost. The French *Deuxième Bureau* (secret service) in Praha received a constant supply of the very latest data on German rearmament, but like the Soviets and the British they didn't bother to reciprocate in any meaningful way.

The glue that held the Czech spy sources in Germany together was a German *Abwehrabteilung* (or simply *Abwehr*) agent named Paul Thümmel, code named A-54. Thümmel was an old Nazi party member stationed in the Abwehr office in Dresden which was responsible for German spy operations against Czechoslovakia. It remains a mystery what it was that "turned" A-54 to work for Moravec, but apparently it was money. He began his work for the Czechs in 1937 when he wrote Moravec a letter in which he offered to sell information regarding German mobilization for cash. Originally suspicious that Thümmel was a double-agent working to penetrate Czech intelligence, Moravec took a great risk and ended up with the sort of spy that all intelligence chiefs dream of.

Shortly after the *"Four-Power Conference"* in München authorized the German absorption of the Sudetenland, Beneš was forced to resign as president and was succeeded by Emil Hácha. At the end of October 1938 Beneš fled Czechoslovakia by flying to London, and from there to the United States.

Fortunately for Col František Moravec, the British SIS still needed him very badly to get to his agent A-54. Their need for intelligence data from a well established German source had never been greater. SIS agreed to provide refuge for Moravec, if and when he ever needed it, in exchange for continued access to the Abwehr agent, A-54.

Early in March of 1939 A-54 provided Moravec with unbelievable news. He claimed that the German army would occupy all of Bohemia and Moravia on the 15th of March and that German police would hunt down the members of Czech military intelligence and eliminate them. Naturally, A-54 was concerned that he would likely be exposed in the subsequent investigations. He too was looking for a safe haven.

After being brushed aside as an alarmist by members of the Hácha Government, Moravec decided to flee Czechoslovakia with his staff and his files. The most sensitive of his intelligence documents left the country in British diplomatic pouches. Explaining to his wife that he was going on an "overnight trip", Moravec took only a small suitcase to the War Ministry where the best of his staff had been gathered. He informed them that they would not be allowed to say goodbye to their families but would accompany him that same afternoon on a KLM flight chartered by SIS station chief in Praha, Major Harold Gibson. After destroying all remaining documents Moravec and his staff made their way to the airport in small groups to avoid detection, just hours ahead of the German invasion.

By the end of July 1939 Beneš had rejoined Moravec in Britain. Moravec and his agent A-54 had made a deal with British SIS to the exclusion of the French *Deuxième Bureau* which had attempted to avail itself of their services. Fortunately for Beneš and Moravec the British were more eager than ever to continue receiving reports emanating from secret agent A-54. It was said that the content of Thümmel's reports was far less important than the impact *simply receiving them* had on SIS and the British government.

With the sudden surrender of France in June of 1940 the country of Britain was faced with an entirely new set of problems and a new agenda. The situation brought about the creation of a new secret British agency, the Special Operations Executive (SOE), which was authorized at the very highest level to use virtually any means to sabotage, subvert and weaken the German enemy. Suddenly, the Czech Home Army that Eduard Beneš had been touting for years began to have some appeal to the British beyond the information they were receiving from A-54 relayed through the Czech underground. The Government of Britain authorized "provisional recognition" for the Czechoslovakian government-in-exile of President Beneš (the exiled governments of the Netherlands and Poland already had *full* diplomatic recognition in Britain).

In an unexpected but very welcome turn of events, Col Moravec's Abwehr agent, Paul Thümmel, had just been transferred from Dresden to Praha and placed in charge of Abwehr operations in the Balkans and the Near East. An existing group of three of Moravec's old agents assumed responsibility for collecting and transmitting A-54s intelligence data to England. The three were Col Mašín, Col Balabán and Capt Morávek (code name OTA, no relation to Col Moravec in London or the safe-house Moravec's in Praha) known collectively under the code name THREE KINGS.

By fall Moravec was working with the SOE as well as the SIS. In Czechoslovakia the *UVOD (Ustřední vedení odboje domácího)*, or Central Council of the Home Resistance surfaced representing all groups except the communists. UVOD was responsible to Beneš for anti-German efforts of three specific types: subtle sabotage of German communications (changing street signs for example), collecting intelligence data, and passive resistance such as work slow-downs. Beneš was long on record as opposing any, "spectacular actions which could provoke reprisals". German reprisals against the Czech universities in the fall of 1939 were very fresh in his mind. During this period the remnants of the Czechoslovakian Brigade which had escaped during the fall of France began to filter into Britain.

On 22 June 1941 the relatively static military and diplomatic situation in Europe was completely upset by the unexpected German invasion of the Soviet Union. Quite naturally, this released the many communists in Czechoslovakia from the uneasy truce they had maintained with German occupation forces while Germany and the Soviet Union had been concluding treaties of friendship. The importance of this change was enormous and was not lost on Beneš or Moravec. They were fearful that a new Soviet-supplied communist underground in Czechoslovakia could win over large numbers of Czech citizens (and perhaps even the Home Army), eroding support for the Beneš government-in-exile in Britain. On the other hand, even partial British diplomatic recognition of the Beneš government was making Beneš and Moravec look good back in Czechoslovakia.

A plan for members of the Czech Brigade in Britain also began to materialize. SOE and Moravec had decided to select a group of 14 officers and a 22 noncommissioned officers to undergo special training to prepare them to be parachuted back into Bohemia and Moravia. They were to take with them the communications equipment and weapons necessary to expand the flow of vital intelligence information, not only from A-54 via the THREE KINGS, but also from the rest of the underground resistance in Czechoslovakia as well. This communications network was to be, "manned by trained military personnel to co-ordinate supply drops [of arms] and provide a link with the British High Command". Moravec wanted a pool of agents to be available by winter when long periods of darkness would provide cover for air-drop flights to Czechoslovakia.

Needing allies anywhere they could find them, the Soviet Union extended full diplomatic recognition to the Beneš government in London at noon on 18 July 1941. Three hours later the British followed suit *carefully avoiding* any agreement to honor the original borders of Czechoslovakia. While these diplomatic moves certainly strengthened Beneš' hand with the resistance at home, they came at a high price: the British and Soviets began pressing Beneš to understand that *a maximum war effort would be required from every country, including Czechoslovakia.*

The first group of Czechoslovakians to undergo special SOE training was actually larger than originally planned. All Czechoslovakian personnel were first sent for refitting and to be organized into units at their base camp at Cholmondeley Park near Chester. Commando (weapons, explosives and hand-to-hand combat) training in Scotland and parachutist training at the Royal Air Force station Wilmslow weeded out many candidates

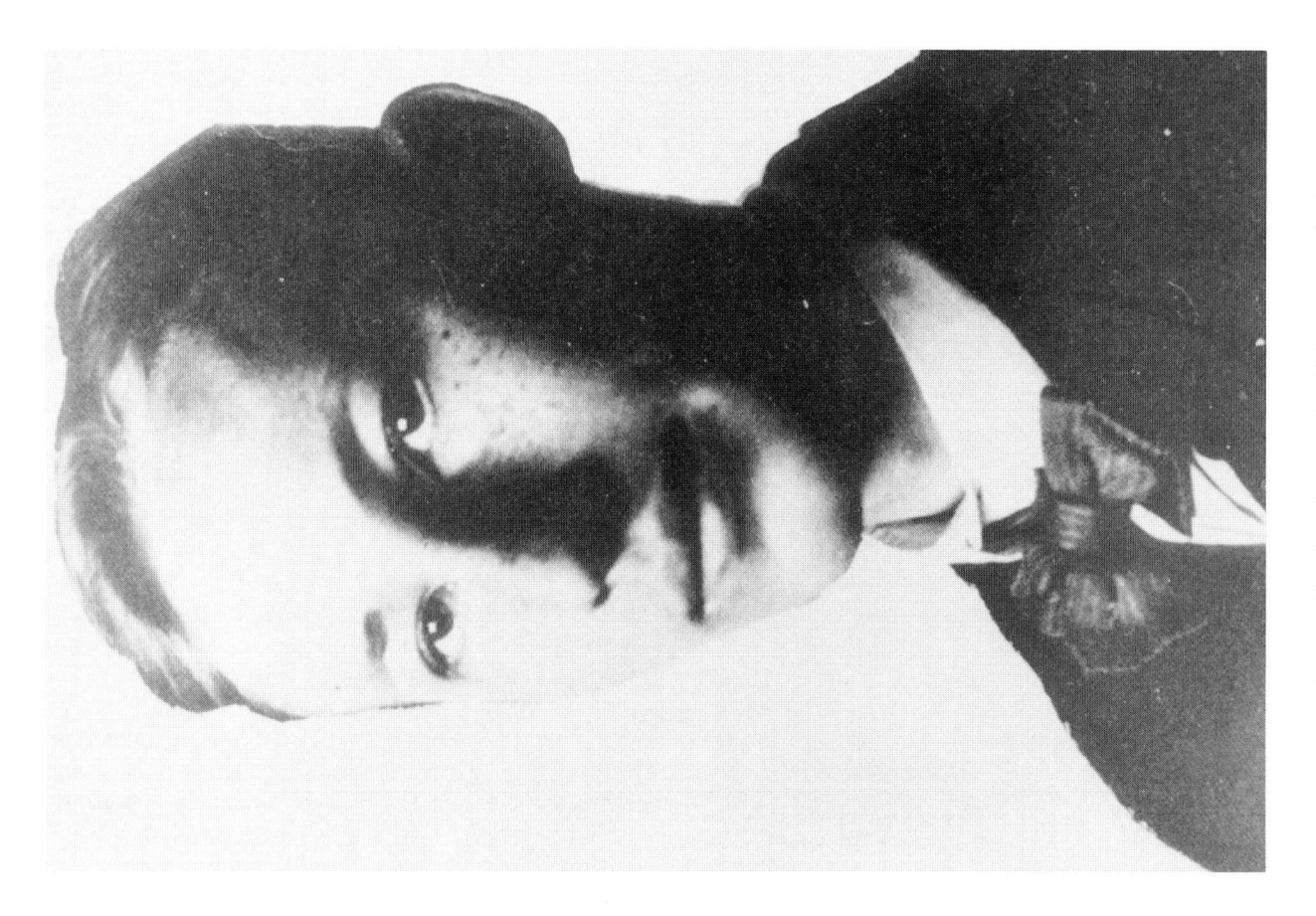

Heydrich was an expert swordsman.

Reinhard Tristan Eugen Heydrich as a student.

prior to the SOE School for Sabotage at Brickendonbury Manor in Hertforshire. Radio operators got special training and most graduates were sent to Villa Bellasis near Dorking, Surrey, for instruction in specific tasks prior to being assigned a mission.

Many operations were planned for the following year which were intended to prove to the British and Soviet governments that Beneš was capable of bringing the Czechoslovakian underground into action. According to Moravec OPERATION ANTHROPOID* would play a key role by, "providing a spark which would activate the mass of the people".

REINHARD HEYDRICH

Reinhard Tristan Eugen Heydrich was born on 07 March 1904 in the building in Halle, Germany which housed his parent's music school. It is reported that at the moment of his birth a group of students was practicing a string quartet in the rehearsal room while another student played a Chopin piece on the piano in an adjoining room. Music was to be very important to Heydrich for the rest of his life.

Reinhard Heydrich was named for the hero of the opera *Amen,* written by his father and first performed in Köln in 1895. He had a sister, Maria, born in 1901 and a brother, Heinz, born in 1905.

Reinhard's father was Richard Bruno Heydrich (known as Bruno Heydrich), a well known and respected musician, composer and the headmaster of the Halle Conservatorium. Bruno's father was Karl Julius Reinhold Heydrich, who had been a cabinet maker employed by the Grotrian-Steinweg Piano Company in Braunschweig and was married to Ernestine Wilhelmine Lindner.

Richard Bruno Heydrich's wife was Elizabeth Maria Anna Amalie Krantz. She was a teacher of voice and piano at the Halle Conservatorium and her father, Professor Dr Eugen Krantz, was Director of the Royal Conservatorium at Dresden. Her mother was Maria Antonie Mautsch.

During his childhood, Reinhard Heydrich was apparently quite a normal boy in most respects but he excelled in music, sports and the humanities. He practiced hard and took instruction well enough to become a competent performer on an array of woodwind, brass and stringed instruments. He did not enjoy losing and rarely lost in sports such as swimming, riding, tennis, fencing and sailing. It seemed virtually certain that the talented, young Reinhard would follow the wishes of his parents and become a *Doctor of Music* at the University in Bonn.

Heydrich was 10 when World War I began and 14 when the Kaiser abdicated and Germany collapsed in 1918. Like a great many young men in Germany at the time he felt betrayed and angry at those he was convinced had sabotaged and humiliated his country in the surrender at the end of the war. At 16 he joined the *Freikorps* in 1920. In this extreme right-wing paramilitary organization he found release for his anger toward Weimar politicians, communists and others without taking allegiance to anyone but the local Freikorps unit commander. The Freikorps considered war to be a normal condition and as a member Heydrich was able to associate with many combat veterans of the World War and had his first exposure to weapons.

In 1921 a girlfriend, Rosa Stapel, introduced Heydrich to a friend of her brother Ernst - Reiner Thiess. Thiess was a naval cadet and Reinhard bombarded him with questions about the sea service.

Heydrich graduated from the Halle Reformgymnasium (the approximate equivalent of an American college preparatory school) in the spring of 1922. By August he was in Kiel to visit Thiess for three weeks and to investigate the possibilities of a naval career. Thiess was serving aboard the cruiser *Berlin* and introduced Heydrich to a Lieutenant Commander aboard the ship, Wilhelm Franz Canaris. A lifelong friendship with

---

OPERATION ANTHROPOID, was composed of Sergeants Josef Gabčík and Jan Kubiš and was parachuted into Czechoslovakia during the early morning hours of 29 December 1941 in a combined flight with *OPERATIONs SILVER A* and *SILVER B*. The assignment accepted by Gabčík and Kubiš prior to departure was to, "at the right time and in the right place and under ideal conditions, perform sabotage or terroristic activity important enough that it will become well known *even outside of* Czechoslovakia". Col František Moravec suggested to Gabčík that they try to kill either Acting Reichsprotektor Reinhard Heydrich or his Secretary of State Karl Frank.

A somber military portrait of Heydrich by Heinrich Hoffmann.

Lina Mathilde von Osten Heydrich and her husband Reinhard.

Canaris began.*

Canaris was born on 01 January 1887 in Aplerbeck near Dortmund, Germany. As a child he was called *"Kieker"* (peeper or snooper) a name that foreshadowed his later career as Chief of the Abwehrabteilung (military intelligence service) during World War II. In spring 1905 Canaris entered the Imperial Naval Academy at Kiel. During World War I while serving in the area of the Falkland Islands aboard the cruiser *Dresden* he was captured and imprisoned by the British on Quiriquina Island near Valparaiso, Chile. He stole a small boat and rowed himself to the mainland, rode horseback over the Andes to Buenos Aires and got aboard the Dutch ship *Frisia* bound for Rotterdam. This incredible adventure was undertaken and finished by Canaris under the assumed name of *Reed Rosas* in fluent Spanish.

After a brief stint in Hamburg, Canaris was sent to Madrid on his first naval intelligence assignment, still using the name Reed Rosas and his fake Chilean passport. While attempting to return to Germany via Italy in February 1916, "Reed Rosas" was arrested as a spy near Domodossola and imprisoned in Genoa. Feigning the desire for conversion, Canaris managed to get the prison Chaplain into his cell, killed him and walked out in the priests clothing before the body was found. Canaris returned to Madrid where he took command of a German submarine.

On 22 November 1919 Canaris married Erika Waag, the sister of a fellow naval officer. By remarkable coincidence Erika Waag had once been a music student of Eugen Krantz at the Royal Conservatorium in Dresden.

The young Heydrich was very impressed with Commander Canaris and his wife, and the Commander convinced Heydrich that he would have a greater future in the navy than in the world of music. Mrs Canaris invited Heydrich to attend her Sunday evening chamber music sessions, and to accompany her on his violin.

Heydrich enlisted in the navy over the objection of his parents and was made a Midshipman on 1 April 1924. By July 1928 he was a signals officer in naval intelligence on the staff of Admiral Erich Raeder in Kiel. Raeder described the ambitious Heydrich as a, "young man with great abilities and far to go". Heydrich's life as a spy was well underway. By 1930 he was promoted to Chief Signals Officer and had attained fluency in English, French and Russian.

One story says that during this period Heydrich had a brief affair with the daughter of I G Farben company director Otto Schlueter. By early 1931 when Miss Schlueter told him she was pregnant with his child, Heydrich was already engaged to marry Nazi party member 1201380, Lina Mathilde von Osten, the 19 year old daughter of a Fehmarn Island schoolmaster. The pregnant girl's father demanded that Heydrich marry her. Heydrich left the matter in the hands of his fiancee by saying that he would not break off his engagement with von Osten so long as she was still willing to marry him. She was.

Otto Schlueter was very well known among the powerful in both civilian and military circles and is said to have gone directly to Admiral Raeder demanding that Raeder force Heydrich to marry his daughter. According to the story, Raeder ordered it and Heydrich refused, setting in motion a Court of Honor that dismissed him from the navy in April 1931. Reinhard Heydrich's own version of this story which he repeated publicly many times, was that he was removed from the navy for "political reasons". No transcript or other official record of a Court of Honor proceeding against Heydrich appears to exist [1994].

On 14 June 1931 Heydrich successfully completed a job interview in München with Reichsführer-*ℋ* Heinrich Himmler who was seeking someone to establish a secret service (*Sicherheitsdienst* or SD) within the *ℋ*. Nazi party member 544916 Heydrich was hired for the job effective 01 October 1931, became *ℋ* member 10120 and was given the rank of Sturmführer-*ℋ* (Lance Corporal). Heydrich and Lina von Osten married in the village church of Grossenbrode on 26 December 1931, apparently unworried about their prospects for the future in a depression-ridden country with millions of unemployed.

Partly because of his navy experience Heydrich possessed a strong background for intelligence work, and his superiors praised his natural abilities as well. He worked with passion to create a central card file on known criminals and suspects,

---

*While many sources have attempted to portray a distant and even competitive relationship between Canaris and Heydrich, I have uncovered *not a single piece* of authentic source material that would indicate that they were anything other than very supportive, dear friends over the course of Heydrich's life.

Himmler, Wolf, Hitler and Heydrich in Praha for the proclomation of the *Protektorate of Bohemia and Moravia* on 16 March 1939. Below, Heydrich, Frank, Himmler and others listened to Hitler in München.

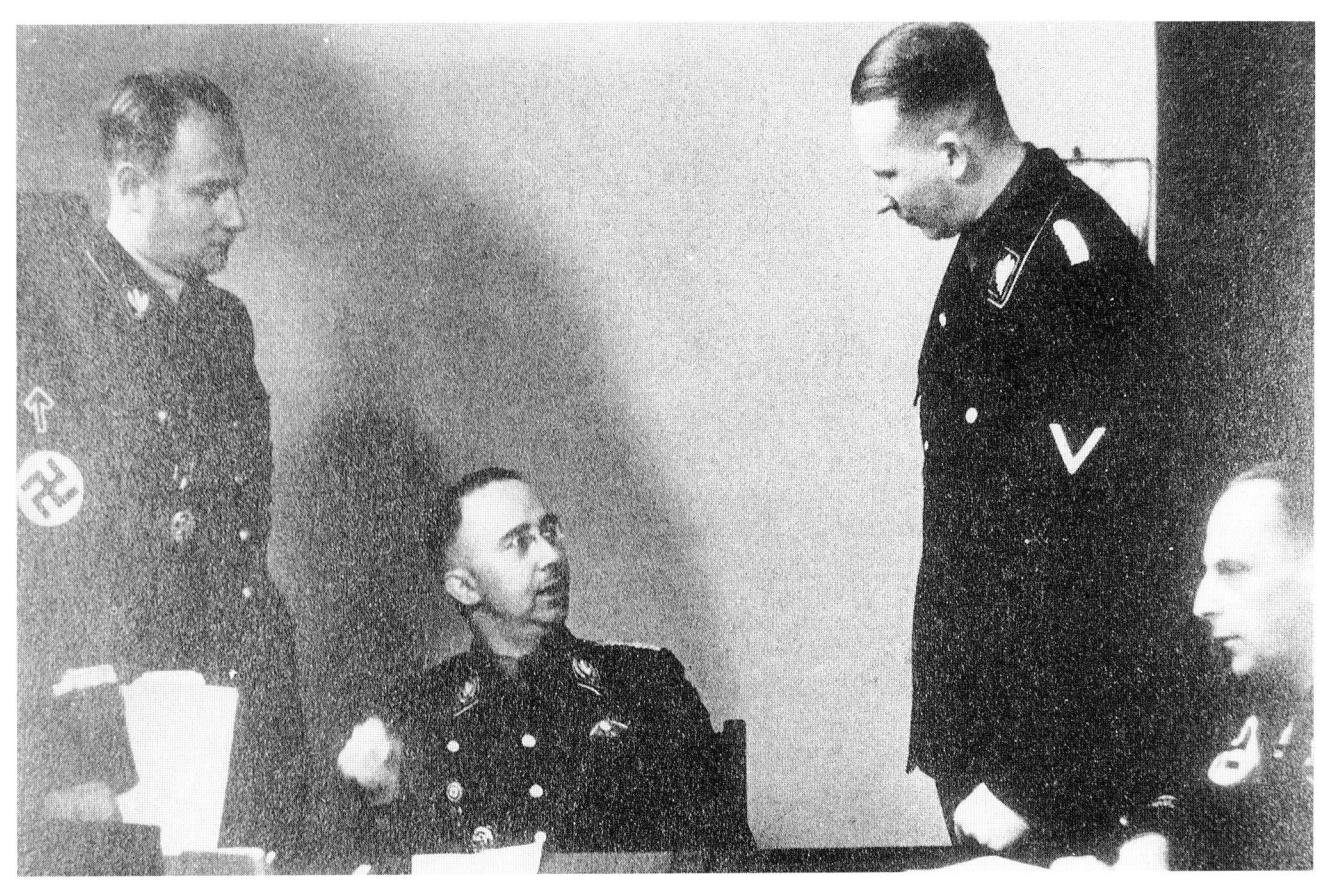

Heydrich speaking with his boss, Reichsführer-SS Heinrich Himmler. Below, SS-Obersturmbahnführer Huber, SS-Oberführer Nebe, Reichsführer-SS Himmler, SS-Gruppenführer Heydrich and SS-Oberführer Müller.

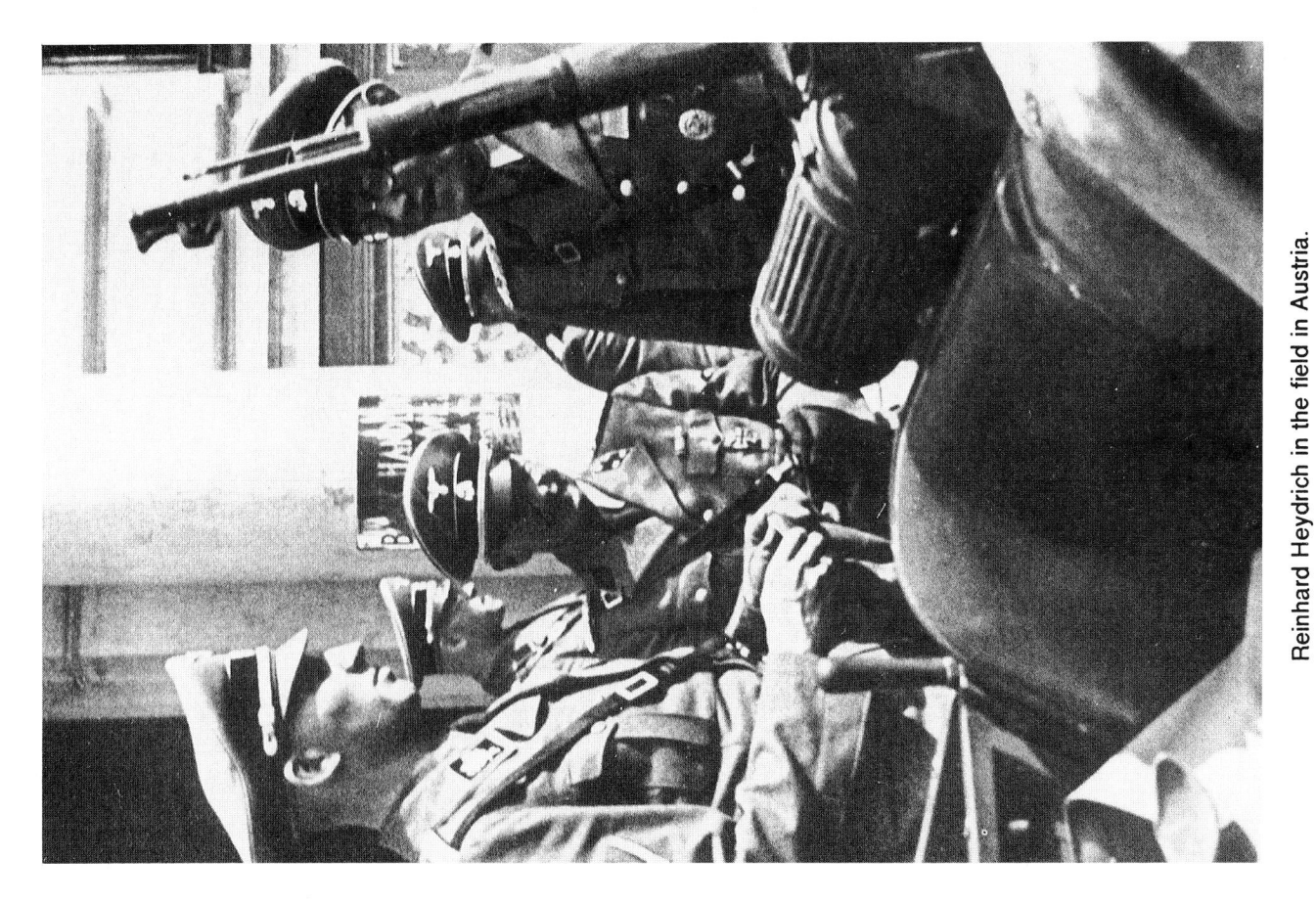

Reinhard Heydrich in the field in Austria.

Himmler visiting with Heydrich.

and he traveled widely recruiting full-time agents. Heydrich was particularly successful in recruiting men for the SD from excellent families with good academic credentials, including his own brother Heinz Siegfried Heydrich.

With the collapse of the Weimar government and the appointment of Hitler as Chancellor of Germany, Heydrich was given a free hand by his boss, Reichsführer-*SS* Heinrich Himmler, to reorganize the German police system. He began in Bavaria in March 1933. In April 1934 Heydrich moved from München to Berlin and played several key roles in the destruction of Ernst Röhm and his SA empire. In 1935 he founded the *SS* newspaper, *Das Schwarze Korps*. Upon the recommendation of Reinhard Heydrich his old mentor, Admiral Wilhelm Canaris was appointed Chief of the Abwehr on 2 January 1935. The Heydrich and Canaris families lived as neighbors in the Berlin suburb of Sudende.

In 1936 Reinhard Heydrich became the head of the Gestapo *(Geheime Staatspolizei)* and the Kripo *(Kriminalpolizei)* which together became the Sipo *(Sicherheitspolizei)*, while retaining his old job as SD Chief. Hitler ordered young Heydrich to turn the 1936 Olympic games in Berlin and Garmisch-Partenkirchen into a Nazi festival. He did a masterful job. By 1939 the headquarters of the Sipo (including the Gestapo and the Kripo) and the SD were combined to form the *Reichssicherheitshauptamt* (RSHA) or Main Office of Reich Security under the leadership of 35 year old *SS-Gruppenführer* Reinhard Heydrich in Berlin. With the establishment of the RSHA Heydrich, while officially subordinate to Himmler, was at last supreme in the field of intelligence gathering. He was free to do as he wished.

Remarkably, one of the first things Heydrich (a Major General in the *SS*) chose to do was to ask Luftwaffe General Loertzer to activate him for service (he was a reserve Captain in the Luftwaffe) so he could fly as an ordinary turret gunner with Bomb Group KG55! His first mission took place on 12 September 1939. Heydrich then began to practice at the air field at Staaken and quickly passed his fighter pilot examination. He saw his first action as a fighter pilot in a ME 109 during the Norwegian campaign. Later he flew photo reconnaissance missions over England and Scotland in a ME 110. Himmler finally grounded Heydrich after he had to be rescued from a crash landing near Bersina at the start of the German invasion of the Soviet Union.

With the vastly larger scale of war in the East the Germans found it essential to get every last turnip from the farms and every last bullet from the factories in occupied Europe. It was common knowledge that productivity in Bohemia and Moravia had never approached 100% under the direction of career diplomat and Reichsprotektor von Neurath. Hitler relieved him on 23 September 1941, placing him on sick leave and citing his need for a vacation.

At the same time Hitler announced that Heydrich had been promoted to *SS-Obergruppenführer* (Lieutenant General) and posted on 27 September to Praha as Acting Reichsprotektor (von Neurath was still the *official* Reichsprotektor for diplomatic reasons) of Bohemia and Moravia. It was expected that the organizational genius of Heydrich could turn things around quickly in Czechoslovakia. Heydrich still retained his permanent job as Chief of RSHA in Berlin and was confident that he could oversee the Reichsprotektor job with the able help of his Secretary of State, *SS*-Gruppenführer Karl H Frank on day-to-day matters in Praha.

Heydrich's stated objective as Acting Reichsprotektor was the, "depoliticisation of the Czech population". In practice that meant an attempt would be made to fully integrate the provinces of Bohemia and Moravia into Germany over time. The largest percentage of the population was to undergo "Germanization" while undesirables were to be identified and deported to make room for the resettlement of their lands by ethnic Germans. In a small but clear demonstration of his intent, Heydrich reopened the nineteenth century German Concert Hall in Praha (it had been in use as the Czechoslovakian Chamber of Deputies) and had Smetana Square renamed in honor of the composer Mozart.

Many of Heydrich's measures were very well received in the Protektorate. Two hundred-thousand pair of shoes were distributed free, and fat and tobacco rations for certain classes of workers were increased substantially. Some of his measures were very severe. Martial law was declared upon his arrival and police sweeps netted thousands of suspects. 404 were convicted of crimes and sentenced to death. Of these, 215 were convicted of political crimes and 189 were convicted of economic crimes such as black marketeering.

The Czechoslovakian Prime Minister, Alois Eliáš

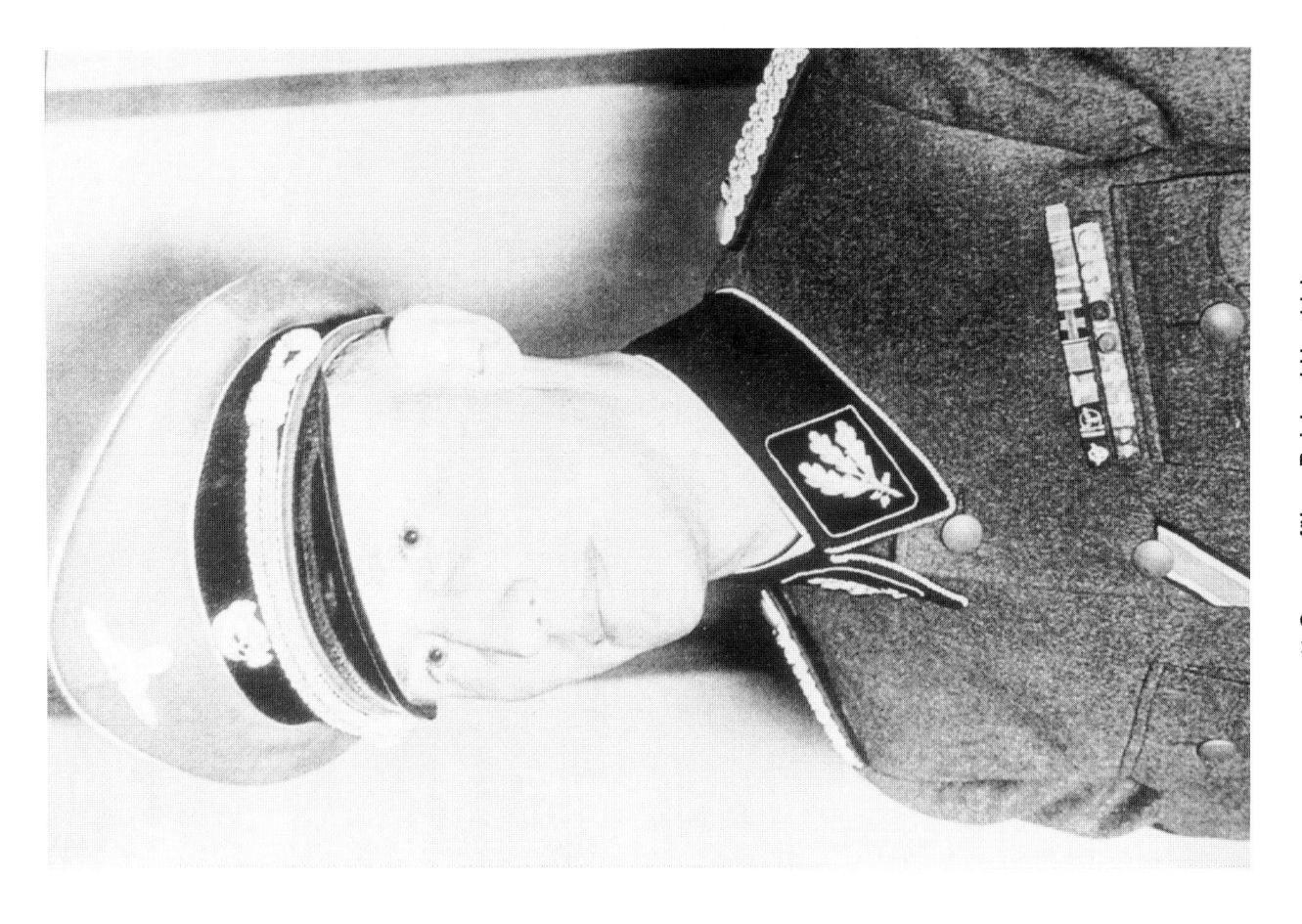

SS-Gruppenführer Reinhard Heydrich.

Reinhard Heydrich - Luftwaffe combat pilot.

Praha looked very normal on the outside.

The Germans occupied Praha on 15 March 1939.

Ethnic Germans in the Sudetenland welcomed the Nazi occupation. Most Czechoslovakians hated it. Below, a huge portrait of Adolf Hitler in front of the Church of Our Lady of Tyn on Praha's Old Town Square.

The Reichsprotektor of Bohemia and Moravia, ✠-Obergruppenführer Reinhard Heydrich and his Secretary of State, ✠-Gruppenführer Karl H Frank.

was arrested for working with the underground, tried and sentenced to death. His sentence was postponed and word was leaked out that he would testify in the trials of other conspirators. This simple ploy caused many in the resistance to rethink their underground roles. All radio links between the Czech underground and their handlers with the SOE and Czechoslovakian government-in-exile in England were cut by the Gestapo. Heydrich publicly laid all blame for the severe measures, the arrests and the executions on, "the resistance that was being orchestrated from Moscow and London".

By 19 January 1942 things had improved for the Acting Reichsprotektor to the extent that martial law was lifted, but the standard work day was lengthened from 8 to 12 hours to increase war production. In April 1942 the social security system was overhauled (increasing benefits by approximately 30%) to bring it into line with the system in Germany. Heydrich called in Hitler's architect, Albert Speer, for recommendations on how he might rebuild Praha as a German city, and

Above, Heydrich on a visit to France in May of 1942. Below, Heydrich reviewed troops in front of Hradčany Castle as he assumed command in Praha on 28 September 1941.

Below, Černinsky Palace in Praha housed Karl Hermann Frank's office. See page 103.

Himmler joined Heydrich for an inspection in Praha on 29 October 1941.

plans were laid to link Praha with the German Autobahn system.

The first seven months of the administration of Acting Reichsprotektor Reinhard Heydrich were highly successful from a German point of view. He had accomplished a great many of his objectives and it seemed that nothing could come between him and success. The German police in Bohemia and Moravia were also having a field-day, intercepting almost every clandestine operation sent out from Britain. (A recap of the most significant of the SOE parachute operations into Czechoslovakia during the Heydrich period in Praha, is provided in appendix B for reference).

In mid-May Heydrich felt comfortable enough with the situation in Praha to leave the Protektorate for a visit in the West to inspect security measures there. While in Paris he attended the installation ceremony for his friend, ⁄⁄-Gruppenführer Karl Oberg as police commander for France.

By the end of May 1942 the only real survivors of SOE air-drop operations in Czechoslovakia that were still at large *and in possession of their equipment* were Josef Gabčík and Jan Kubiš of OPERATION ANTHROPOID (28/29 December 1941) and they were in hiding in Praha. With the assistance of a few brave comrades they continued to plan the murder of Reinhard Heydrich.

Below, Adolf Hitler speaks with Arthur Seyss-Inquart while Reinhard Heydrich looks on.

Under the gaze of the Führer, Heydrich charmed the ladies.

SS-Obergruppenführer Reinhard Heydrich and SS-Gruppenführer Karl Frank. Below, Heydrich spoke with Czech farmers on 5 January 1942.

Heydrich speaking in the historic Czech Music Hall in Praha on 16 October 1941.

Heydrich making an inspection at the Reich Security School.

Czechoslovakian President Eduard Beneš decorated Gabčík *(L)* and Kubiš *(R)* for bravery during the Battle of France in 1940. Below, with less than 6 months to live - Kubiš *(L)* and Gabčík *(R)* on 18 December 1941.

THE PARACHUTISTS

THE AIR DROP

On 28 December 1941 Gabčík and Kubiš of OPERATION ANTHROPOID boarded a specially converted Halifax bomber at Tangmere (England) Airfield at 22:00. The plane, which departed almost at once, was piloted by RAF Flight Lieutenant Ron C Hockey and also carried the five Czech parachutists of OPERATIONS SILVER A and SILVER B. At about 22:50 the Halifax crossed the French coast flying almost straight east. About 01:30 on the 29th it passed by Bayreuth, Germany and arrived over the fog shrouded drop-zone near Plzeň, Czechoslovakia at 02:15. Gabčík and Kubiš bailed out about ten minutes later from 900 feet (275 meters).

Gabčík and Kubiš had missed their drop-zone by a wide margin when they jumped over Czechoslovakia. Instead of landing in forests near the Borek airfield at Plzeň they landed in open ground many miles to the northeast near the small village of Nehvizdy, 20 miles from Praha. Gabčík injured his foot in landing on the frozen ground.

After the two buried their parachutes in the snow they began a reconnaissance to determine where they were and to find a safe place to hide their equipment. It was immediately obvious to them that they were nowhere near their intended drop-zone. They soon located a shed in which they hid their equipment, eating a small meal from their rations. Continuing, they found an abandoned stone quarry, made themselves comfortable and waited for daylight.

A local gamekeeper, Alois Smejkal, alerted by the noise of the low flying Halifax, started a limited search of his area and quickly located not only the buried parachutes but Gabčík and Kubiš' equipment and the remains of their meal. The carelessly discarded material included a tin food can with a British label! Footprints in the snow quickly led Smejkal to Gabčík and Kubiš.

Fortunately, the trio was soon located by a fourth man, a local miller and Sokol member with close ties to the underground resistance. The miller passed Gabčík and Kubiš through to a second Sokol member, Ladislav Vaněk (code name JINDRA) who took them to Praha and interrogated them to assure himself they were not Gestapo agents trying to infiltrate the underground resistance.

Satisfied they were who they claimed to be JINDRA passed Gabčík and Kubiš to underground operative Jan Zelenka (cover name HAJASKY), safe-house specialist for people on the run from the authorities. He found a doctor to treat Gabčík's foot and provided new identity documents and medical certificates that exempted the holders from regular work. HAJASKYs expertise proved to be a critical piece of luck as the documents supplied to Gabčík and Kubiš by SOE in England contained blatant errors which would have been obvious to the first policeman that would have examined them.

After a series of moves for security reasons Gabčík and Kubiš ended up in the safe-house apartment of the family Moravec on Biskupova Street in the Praha suburb of Zizkov. "Aunt Marie" Moravec, her railwayman husband and 21 year old son Ata took good care of Gabčík and Kubiš and never pressed them to explain their mission. In the end of February 1942 Gabčík and Kubiš were finally located by Josef Valčík of OPERATION SILVER A, and word was passed back to London through Lieutenant Alfred Bartoš that the ANTHROPOID agents were still alive.

Jan Kubiš and Josef Gabčík spent several months in the underground resistance in Czechoslovakia awaiting the right moment for their assassination attempt on Reinhard Heydrich. They listened carefully to instructions sent by radio and via other parachutists that made their way through the underground. They participated in other operations, such as the very risky CANNONBURY RAID, and met many in the resistance that offered to help them in any way they could. They also took the time to normalize their lives by finding female companions. Gabčík is said to have been engaged to marry the younger daughter (Libena) of the Fafka family and Kubiš was involved with Anna Malinova, a friend of "Aunt Marie" Moravec. They continued to be extremely tight-lipped about the nature of their mission. When asked what they were up to, they claimed to be "counting the ducks in the Vltava River".

The presence of a traitor or traitors in their midst was well known to the Germans. The content of a mountain of data collected by the Praha Gestapo led them to conclude that the information being leaked through the Czech resistance *could*

The Czechoslovakian Brigade being reviewed in England.

Above, Czechoslovakian paratrooper Jan Kubiš is fourth from right. Below, passing through the gates of Cholmondeley Park near Chester, England.

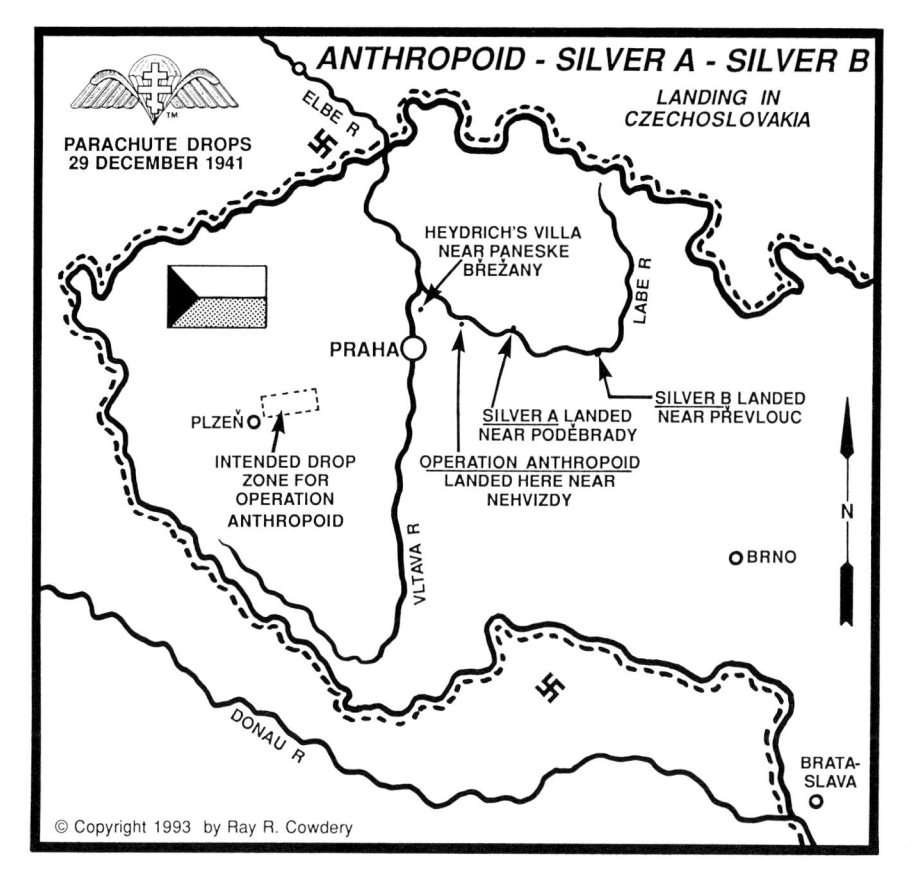

ANTHROPOID - SILVER A - SILVER B
LANDING IN CZECHOSLOVAKIA
PARACHUTE DROPS 29 DECEMBER 1941

- HEYDRICH'S VILLA NEAR PANESKE BŘEŽANY
- PRAHA
- SILVER B LANDED NEAR PŘEVLOUC
- SILVER A LANDED NEAR PODĚBRADY
- OPERATION ANTHROPOID LANDED HERE NEAR NEHVIZDY
- PLZEŇ — INTENDED DROP ZONE FOR OPERATION ANTHROPOID
- BRNO
- BRATASLAVA

© Copyright 1993 by Ray R. Cowdery

only have come from one of three possible suspects: Secretary of State Karl Frank, Head of the Praha Gestapo Dr Hans Geschke or Abwehr agent Paul Thümmel. Thümmel had been arrested by the Gestapo on 13 October 1941 but cleverly avoided detention by boldly challenging his captors to make his arrest public information. Knowing that he was a highly regarded Abwehr officer with very solid connections inside the Nazi party, the Gestapo apologized and dropped the charges on 25 November.

Reinhard Heydrich remained convinced of Thümmels guilt and had him kept under constant police surveillance. On 22 February 1942 Thümmel was rearrested and given a more comprehensive interrogation in complete secrecy. This time he admitted certain dealings with the Czech resistance, but claimed the dealings were related to an Abwehr operation. Knowing they had the right man, the Gestapo released Thümmel and tailed him constantly. On 20 March 1942 he was arrested for the last time. The next day the Gestapo staked out a Praha park awaiting "Three Kings" Capt Morávek who was expected to keep an appointment with Paul Thümmel. Following and exchange of over 50 gunshots, two of which wounded Morávek, he shot himself in the head and fell dead in the gutter of a tram stop near the park entrance. Paul Thümmel was quietly incarcerated in the prison of Terezín (Theresienstadt) under a false identity and was executed by the ⚡⚡ on 27 April 1945, only about a week before the German surrender.

Among Capt Morávek's effects the Gestapo quickly found photos of Bartoš, Valčík and Potůček and each was stamped on the back with the name of a photographer in Pardubice. The photos had been given to Morávek by Alfred Bartoš so that Morávek could supply SILVER A parachutists with new identity papers. The photos were immediately circulated to all police in Czechoslovakia and it forced the three even further underground. Valčík dyed his hair, grew a moustache and moved into the Moravec flat in Zizkov where he was reunited with Gabčík and Kubiš. Although it was a serious infraction of SOE security regulations to do so, Gabčík and Kubiš decided they needed a third, and perhaps a fourth man for their attempt on the life of the Acting Reichsprotektor, so they recruited Josef Valčík.

It was in this very dangerous environment that Gabčík and Kubiš pressed their efforts to find a way to get close enough to Reinhard Heydrich to murder him. Naturally, the comings and goings of the senior police and secret service agent in the country were not public information. Inquiries regarding Heydrich's lifestyle and movements would have been almost certain to arouse suspicion and could have easily revealed the nature of the mission of OPERATION ANTHROPOID. Because he lived outside of Praha and held other jobs outside of Czechoslovakia, Reinhard Heydrich's daily routine was anything but regular.

In an effort to determine more about the routine observed by Heydrich, Gabčík and Kubiš had Zelenka introduce them to Františék Šefařík, a maintenance carpenter working on the staff at Hradčany Castle where Heydrich's Praha office was located. Each evening two women living in the neighborhood below Hradčany would approach the window of a nearby building, and if information regarding Heydrich's daily routine was

Czechoslovakian forces in England were equipped with a variety of British and American equipment.

Combat training in England. Below, parachuting near Manchester.

Good friends - great soldiers, Gabčík and Kubiš. Below, the flag of the *Czechoslovakian-American Sokol* greeted Winston Churchill and Eduard Beneš during an inspection of the Czechoslovakian Brigade.

to be had Šefařík would pass a note to them through the window. A second source of information (unknown to Šefařík) was Josef Novotny, horologist at Hradčany who kept all the clocks in the castle running in an orderly manner. At virtually all times he had free access to all of the offices within the castle complex and was careful to observe people, papers and equipment in use there. There is also little doubt that Gabčík and Kubiš were also receiving data regarding Heydrich's daily routine from the gardener and others on Heydrich's domestic staff at his home in Panenské Břežany, just 15 miles north of Praha.

After great consideration Gabčík and Kubiš narrowed their plans to either an ambush of Heydrich's special train on which he frequently traveled to Berlin, or an attack on his car as it made its way into Praha from his home. The latter plan was adopted and it became only a matter of selecting the proper time and the best spot *en route* to carry it out.

Gabčík and Kubiš' contacts in Hradčany Castle had told them that Heydrich would leave Praha for Berlin on 27 May following a morning visit to his office in the castle. They decided 27 May would be a good time to carry out their mission.

Broadcast and receiving desk of Czechoslovakian Military Radio Central in England.

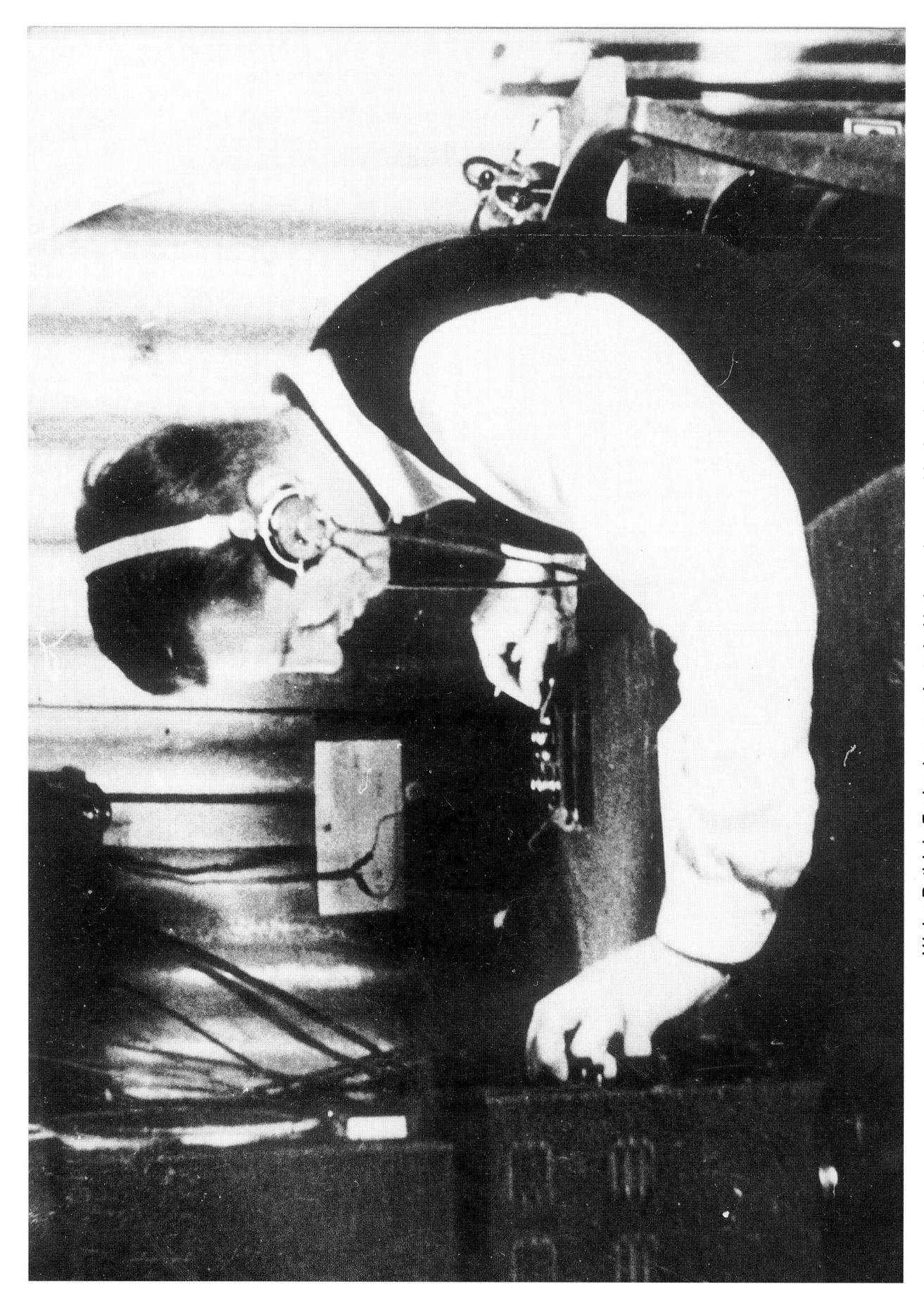

Václav Retich in England communicated with the underground in Czechoslovakia.

Czechoslovakian parachutists in training in Manchester. Below, a part of the *Soldier's Service Book* of Josef Gabčík.

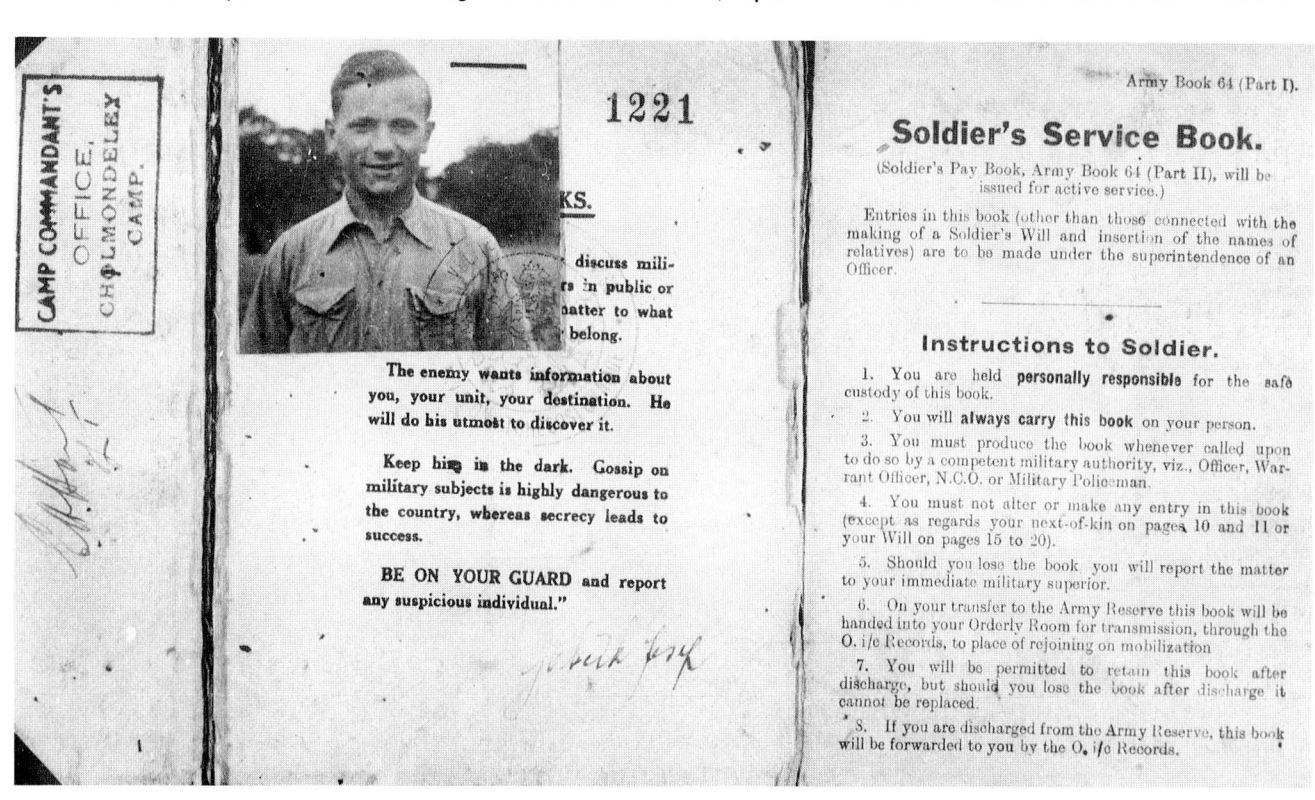

Ron Hockey

Above, Gabčík *(L)* and Kubiš *(R)* photographed in front of the famous "brick wall" of the Porchester Gate in London. Right, Pilot Ron Hockey at the controls of the *Halifax* that transported the parachutists back to Czechoslovakia.

Facing page, the 138th Squadron *Halifax Bomber* number NF-V L9613 which delivered OPERATION ANTHROPOID parachutists to Czechoslovakia was flown by a British/Canadian crew. *L-R*, Pilot Flight Lieutenant Ron C Hockey, Flying Officer Dick Wilkin, Flying Sgt Holden, Flying Sgt Burke, Sgt Hughes, Sgt Berwich, Sgt Walton, unidentified. Capt Hockey was the only crew member to survive WWII. On the 50th Anniversary of the death of Gabčík and Kubiš, Hockey placed flowers in the Church of Saints Cyril and Methodius in Praha. He died shortly thereafter in England.

A rare picture of the Intelligence Staff of the Czechoslovakian Government-in-Exile assembled in England: *L-R* are Col František Moravec, Alois Frank, Jaroslav Stuchlý, Vladimír Cigna, Josef Tauer and Alois Čáslovka. They probably planned the killing of Reinhard Heydrich.

THE ASSASSINATION ATTEMPT

Gabčík and Kubiš had often looked for the most logical spot along Heydrich's route from his home at Panenské Břežany to his office in Praha that would allow them to escape after attempting to kill him. They decided on a hairpin turn between Kirchmeyerstraße and Klein Holeschowitzerstraße that Heydrich regularly had to pass through in the Praha suburb of Kobilisi. Having observed the location on several occasions they noted that all traffic slowed to a snail's pace while negotiating the curve. The corner even had a tram stop that could provide ordinary Czechs with a reason to wait there, and from the corner one had the opportunity to escape in any one of several directions.

It was decided that Kubiš would carry two extremely powerful hand grenades, each packed with one pound (0.4 kg) of gelatinous nitroglycerine, in a briefcase. Gabčík took a 9mm British MKII Sten gun (a submachine gun with detachable stock), with an extra clip of bullets, and another grenade in his briefcase. Each was armed with a .32 caliber Colt pistol.

Riding bicycles, the two reached the corner on Kirchmeyerstraße in Kobilisi at about 08:30 on 27 May, where Josef Valčík of SILVER A and Adolf Opálka of OUT DISTANCE were already waiting. The plan was for Opálka to maintain a lookout to the south of Kirchmayerstraße while Valčík would position himself about a block north of the corner waiting with a mirror to signal the approach of Heydrich's car. Gabčík would stand at the center of the inside of the curve with the Sten gun under a raincoat while Kubiš waited a short distance further on with the grenades in his briefcase. Leaning their bicycles against nearby lampposts they awaited the expected arrival of Heydrich's car at about 09:30. At 10:00 the four paratroopers were still waiting.

Meanwhile, at Panenské Břežany Heydrich and his driver, ⚡Oberscharführer Johannes Klein had

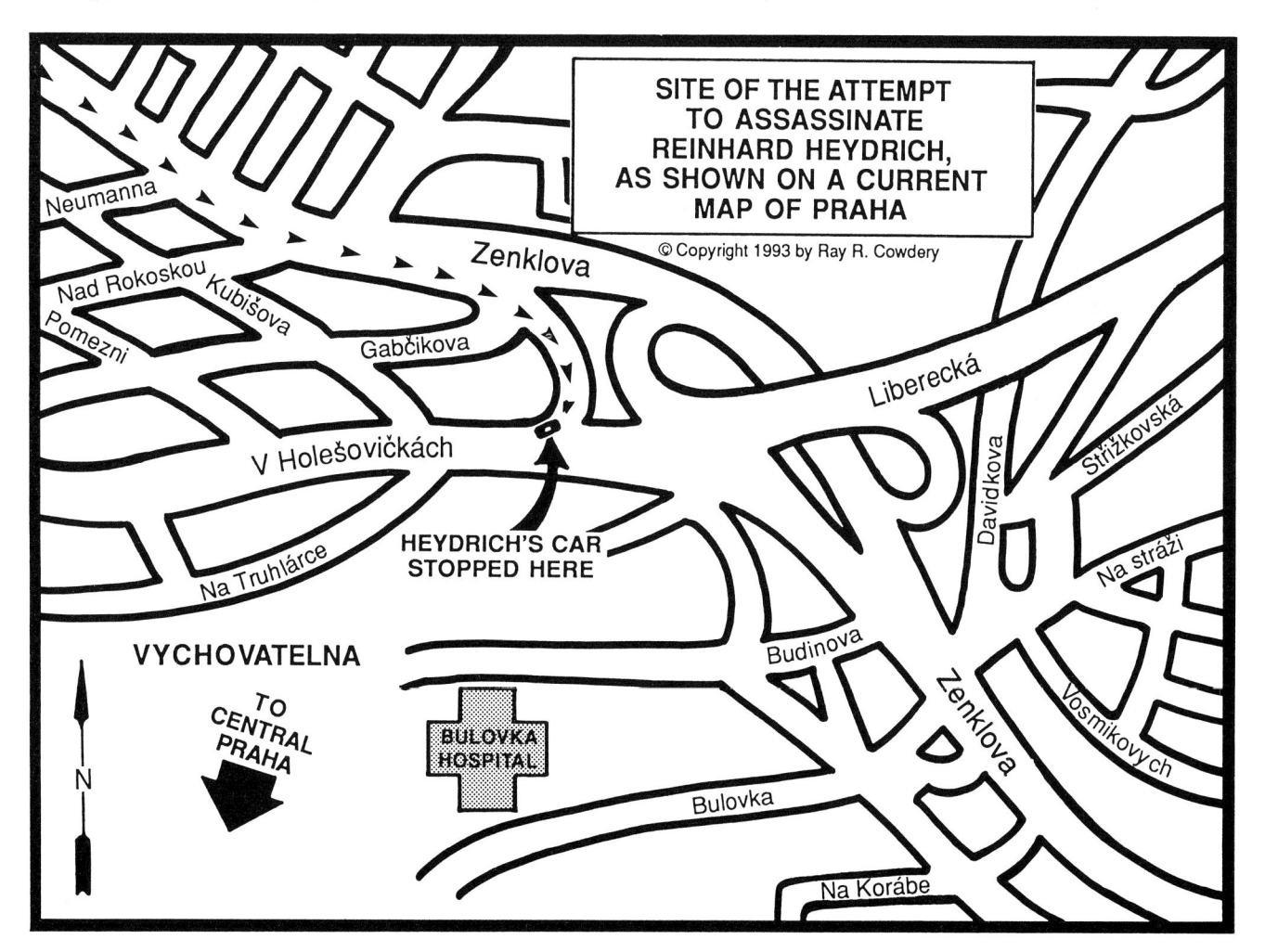

SITE OF THE ATTEMPT TO ASSASSINATE REINHARD HEYDRICH, AS SHOWN ON A CURRENT MAP OF PRAHA

© Copyright 1993 by Ray R. Cowdery

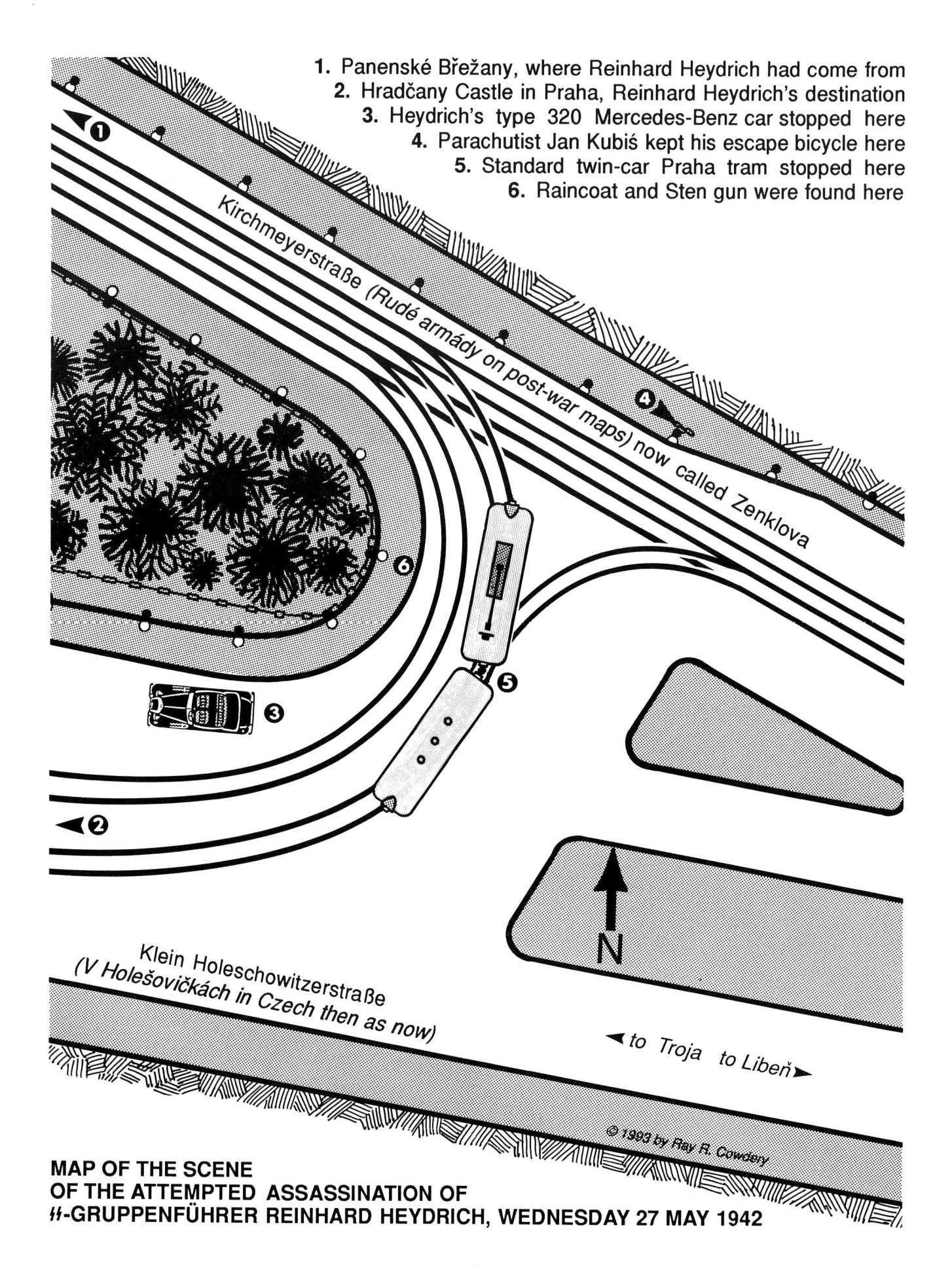

1. Panenské Břežany, where Reinhard Heydrich had come from
2. Hradčany Castle in Praha, Reinhard Heydrich's destination
3. Heydrich's type 320 Mercedes-Benz car stopped here
4. Parachutist Jan Kubiś kept his escape bicycle here
5. Standard twin-car Praha tram stopped here
6. Raincoat and Sten gun were found here

Kirchmeyerstraße (Rudé armády on post-war maps) now called Zenklova

Klein Holeschowitzerstraße
(V Holešovičkách in Czech then as now)

◄ to Troja   to Libeň ►

© 1993 by Ray R. Cowdery

**MAP OF THE SCENE
OF THE ATTEMPTED ASSASSINATION OF
SS-GRUPPENFÜHRER REINHARD HEYDRICH, WEDNESDAY 27 MAY 1942**

50

This photograph of Heydrich's car showed the damage caused by Kubiš' grenade. The license plate number (SS-3) was removed from the photo by the Germans.

Two views of Heydrich's car at the spot it stopped. Above, looking west. Below, looking east.

52

A German photo taken shortly after the assassination attempt shows Heydrich's dark green Mercedes-Benz where it came to a halt along the north side of Klein Holeschowitzerstraße. The spot is easily found yet because the electrical utilities building in the background is still there. Bulovka Hospital is just over the hill behind the electrical building.

just gotten underway, in no particular hurry as they enjoyed the perfect spring weather. The paratroopers paced nervously as they began to imagine that the time they had loitered on the corner was obvious to everyone that passed by. Suddenly, at 10:30 Gabčík saw the glint of sunlight reflecting off Valčík's mirror. Heydrich's car was approaching!

As the dark-green open Mercedes Benz with the ⚡-3 license plate slowed to round the curve off Kirchmeyerstraße and onto Klein Holeschowitzerstraße, Gabčík dropped the raincoat covering his Sten gun, stepped into the street aimed the cocked weapon at Heydrich (sitting in the passenger seat) and pulled the trigger. Nothing happened. The Sten gun malfunctioned and failed to fire.

Watching in disbelief as the car rolled past Gabčík, Kubiš immediately ran toward it and tossed one of his grenades which exploded on contact at running board height. The force of the explosion tore away parts of the right rear fender and running board, damaged the door and blew a large hole in the rear quarter-panel. Kubiš was showered with fragments and bloodied by the explosion.

At once the quiet intersection was transformed into chaos, to the amazement of the panic-stricken passengers on a waiting tram. Heydrich and his driver Klein leapt from the Mercedes just as Kubiš jumped on his bicycle and peddled away in the direction of the city. Gabčík threw down his Sten gun and ran up Kirchmeyerstraße closely followed by Klein with his pistol drawn. As the shots rang out Gabčík turned left onto Kolingartenstraße (now Gabčíkova Street) and darted into Brauner's Butcher Shop on the corner of Pomezi Street. In the ensuing gun battle Gabčík wounded Klein in the thigh and although pursued by Brauner and others, disappeared into the city. Valčík and Opálka fled in opposite directions.

The force of the explosion of the grenade as it tore through the side of the Mercedes had blown debris through the back of the passenger seat, penetrating Heydrich's uniform and body. He was in great pain and somewhat disoriented, but fully conscious as he jumped from the Mercedes. A German woman passing by took charge at the scene, commandeering a truck in which Heydrich was laid on his stomach in the back, atop the cargo.

It took only minutes to reach Bulovka Hospital about half a mile away. There, Heydrich stripped to the waist and allowed Dr Vladimir Snajdr to examine him while Professor Dick, the German resident at Bulovka was summoned. Snajdr, after probing the wound concluded it was probably not particularly dangerous - it did not touch Heydrich's spine or kidneys. On his arrival Professor Dick tended to agree with Snajdr but had Heydrich wheeled to the X-ray room to get a better idea of the damage. Heydrich walked from the wheelchair to the X-ray machine by himself.

The X-ray clearly showed a broken rib and debris in the wound to such an extent that surgery was essential, and Professor Dick proposed it to Heydrich. Heydrich refused, demanding that a surgeon be brought to Praha from Berlin. Dick finally convinced Heydrich that an immediate operation was necessary, and Professor Hollbaum of the German Surgical Clinic of Praha was called in to do it. In the meantime the ⚡ had sealed off the hospital and the floor on which Heydrich was kept, as Karl Frank, Emil Hácha and other dignitaries gathered below. No Czech ever saw Heydrich alive again but according to the German doctors that attended him, the operation went well and the prognosis for a complete recovery was excellent.

THE AFTERMATH - 27 MAY 1942

Shock ran through high ranking military, diplomatic and police circles in Praha as news of the attempt to murder Reinhard Heydrich spread. Just after noon German Secretary of State for Bohemia and Moravia Karl Frank succeeded in reaching Adolf Hitler by phone to inform him. Hitler was outraged to hear that Heydrich was traveling unescorted in an open car when attacked. He immediately ordered reprisals. Hitler instantly appointed Frank as the Interim Reichsprotektor and offered a reward of 1,000,000 RM (US$400,000.00) for the capture, or information which resulted in the capture of the attackers. Hitler further ordered the arrest of 10,000 Czech hostages (to be executed) and the imposition of a sentence of death upon the *entire family* of anyone aiding the

The drivers side of Heydrich's car. Below, the last view Heydrich had before rounding the corner where Gabčík and Kubiš were waiting at 10:30.

This aerial view of the tram and car is looking to the northwest up Kirchmayerstraße (called Rudé armády on post-war maps and now called Zenklova) the direction from which Heydrich had come. Compare with the map on page 50.

A ground level photo of the tram and Heydrich's car, looking southwest.

Gabčík's abandoned bicycle on the north side of Kirchmayerstraße. Below, across the street the Germans found the British Sten gun that failed to function.

Brauner's Butcher Shop where Gabčík shot it out with Heydrich's driver, ⚡-Oberscharführer Johannes Klein. While no longer a butcher shop the place still looks virtually the same.

perpetrators of the attack.

As more than 20,000 police began their search for Gabčík, Kubiš, Opálka and Valčík, the parachutists headed underground. The scene of the attack was carefully examined by German police for the tiniest pieces of evidence. Residents of nearby houses were interrogated by the Gestapo, as were all the tram passengers and on-lookers still at the scene. At 16:30 Interim Reichsprotektor Frank issued his first radio proclamation in both German and Czech, explaining what had happened and the measures that would be taken by the authorities to bring Heydrich's attackers to justice. He announced a 21:00-06:00 curfew, effective at once, which would close all streets and places of leisure and entertainment during nighttime hours. At 21:32 a state-of-siege was proclaimed throughout the Protektorate and every street in Praha was occupied as a house-to-house police sweep of the city began. During the night 541 people were arrested with 111 being remanded to custody for further interrogation. The solitary "notable" among those arrested during the night was Jan Zika, a Czechoslovakian communist party central committeeman.

On the morning of 28 May much of the evidence

Some of the items abandoned by the parachutists after the attempt to kill Heydrich were on display the next morning in the window of the *Bat'a Shoe Store* at 6 Václavském náměstí (Wenceslas Square) in central Praha. These included a beige raincoat, a cap, two brown briefcases and a *Moto-Velo* bicycle. Huge crowds gathered to have a look and to read about the 10,000,000 Czech Crowns (about $350,000.00) offered as a reward for information that would lead to arrests of the perpetrators. The reward was doubled to K20,000,000 on 30 June 1942 when the Czech Government matched the German reward.

collected at the scene of the assassination attempt was put on display in a window of the Bat'a shoe store at 6 Václavském náměstí in the busy heart of Praha. Huge signs offering 10,000,000 Czechoslovakian Crowns (about $350,000) as a reward for information leading to the arrest of Heydrich's attackers attracted enormous crowds of passers-by.

Based on the Sten gun, British grenades and other evidence found at the scene of the crime the Gestapo concluded that the attackers would likely turn out to be parachutists that had come from England, rather than members of a Czechoslovakian resistance or underground group. If they were right, they reasoned that it made no sense to arrest and execute 10,000 Czechoslovakian hostages as Hitler had ordered. Executing 10,000 Czechoslovakians would only do two things for sure: It would decrease production by the output of 10,000 Czechoslovakian workers, and it would create another 75,000 enemies for Germany out of the relatives of those who were executed. Karl Frank left for Germany to try to convince Hitler that there were other methods of dealing with the Czechoslovakians that would yield better results.

The Ministry of Education began a propaganda campaign aimed at convincing Czechoslovakians that loyalty to Germany was an absolute requirement, and that it was nonsense to see Bohemia and Moravia destroyed for the sake of exiled President Beneš and his British handlers. All residents of the Protektorate over fifteen years of age were required to reregister with the police. Anyone not registered by 30 May and all those with whom an unregistered person lived, were to be shot. More than 150 violators of the registration law were apprehended and shot in the first three days of June. These included the parents and relatives of paratrooper Ivan Kolařík (OUT DISTANCE) and the brothers of Arnošt Mikš (ZINC).

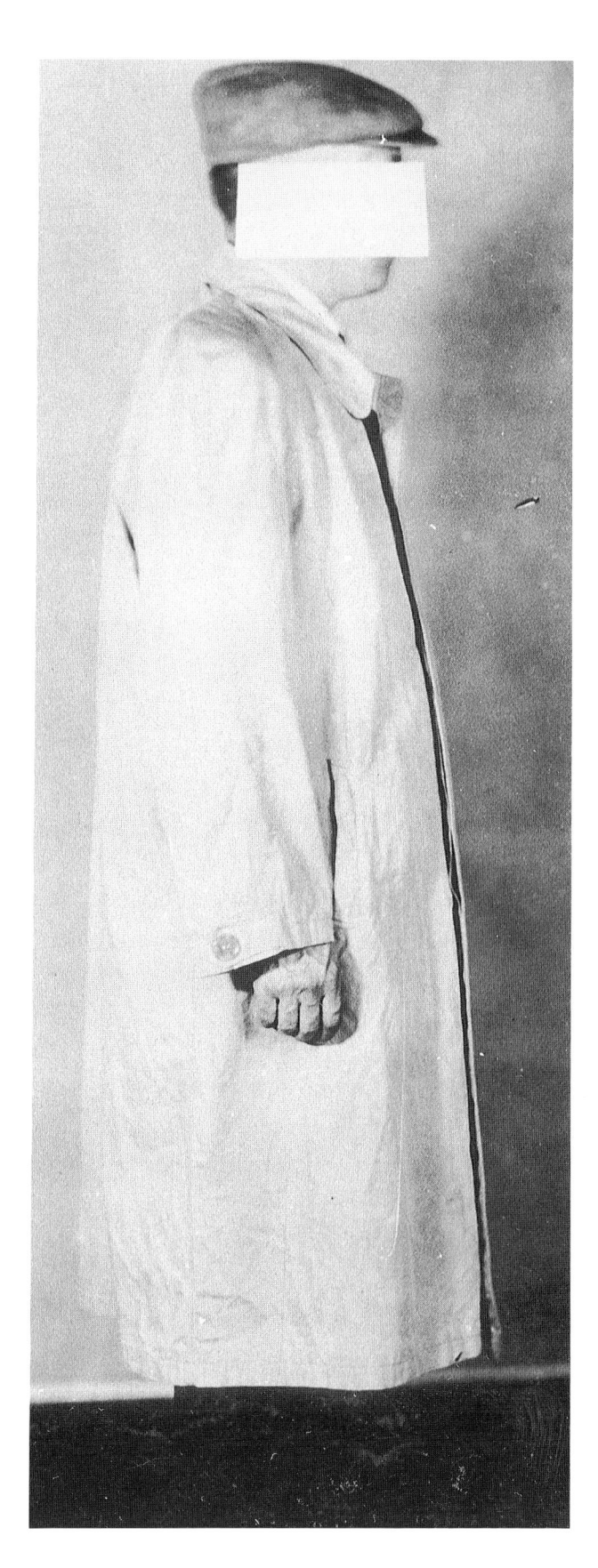

The cap belonged to Kubiš and the raincoat had been used by Gabčík to cover the Sten gun.

On the advice of Frank, Hitler relented and agreed to allow the matter to be handled within the Protektorate. On 30 May Czechoslovakian President Emil Hácha doubled the reward for information leading to the arrest Heydrich's attackers by offering a second 10,000,000 Crowns. The total reward had grown to an amount that must have seemed incredible for the time - the equivalent of $700,000.00!

Heydrich's four attackers meanwhile, were certain their mission had failed and only wished to get as far underground as possible. After reaching safehouses Gabčík, Kubiš, Opálka and Valčík did what they could to alter their appearance and kept moving to safety. In the house-to-house sweep by the Gestapo during the night of the 27th two of the parachutists came within inches of being captured. Leaving Praha was virtually impossible due to new security measures imposed by the Germans. Some way had to be found to get the parachutists to a secure spot where they could stay until the excitement about the attempt on the life of Reinhard Heydrich died down.

The way was finally opened when Jan Zelenka asked Jan Sonnevend, Dean of the Orthodox Church in Praha for help. Sonnevend got the OK from the Priest of the Orthodox Cathedral of Saints Cyril and Methodius, Dr Vladimír Petrék, that parachutists could be kept in the crypt there. In front of the alter officials and clerics of the church took an oath of secrecy regarding the matter. By 01 June seven parachutists had taken refuge in the crypt. They were Valčík (SILVER A), Švarc (TIN), Bublík and Hrubý (BIOSCOP), Opálka (OUT DISTANCE), and Kubiš and Gabčík of ANTHROPOID. Obvious by his absence was Karel Čurda (OUT DISTANCE) who had made his way to southern Bohemia and was in hiding in his mother's barn. While the church crypt was not comfortable, it was safe and quiet and certainly well outside of the suspicion of the Gestapo.

Beyond the borders of Czechoslovakia the rest of the world began to hear about the attempt on the life of Reinhard Heydrich. By radio from Moscow the Czechoslovakian communist Klement Gottwald complimented the "unknown heroes" who had attacked Heydrich, while similar comments emanated from the Beneš camp in Britain. Overjoyed by the demonstration of courage by the Czechoslovakians, the world held its breath awaiting a reaction from Berlin.

Heydrich's doctors prognosis had also proved wrong. His condition had not improved but had ac-

Portrait of Reinhard Heydrich in a SS uniform.

The Death Mask of Reinhard Heydrich.

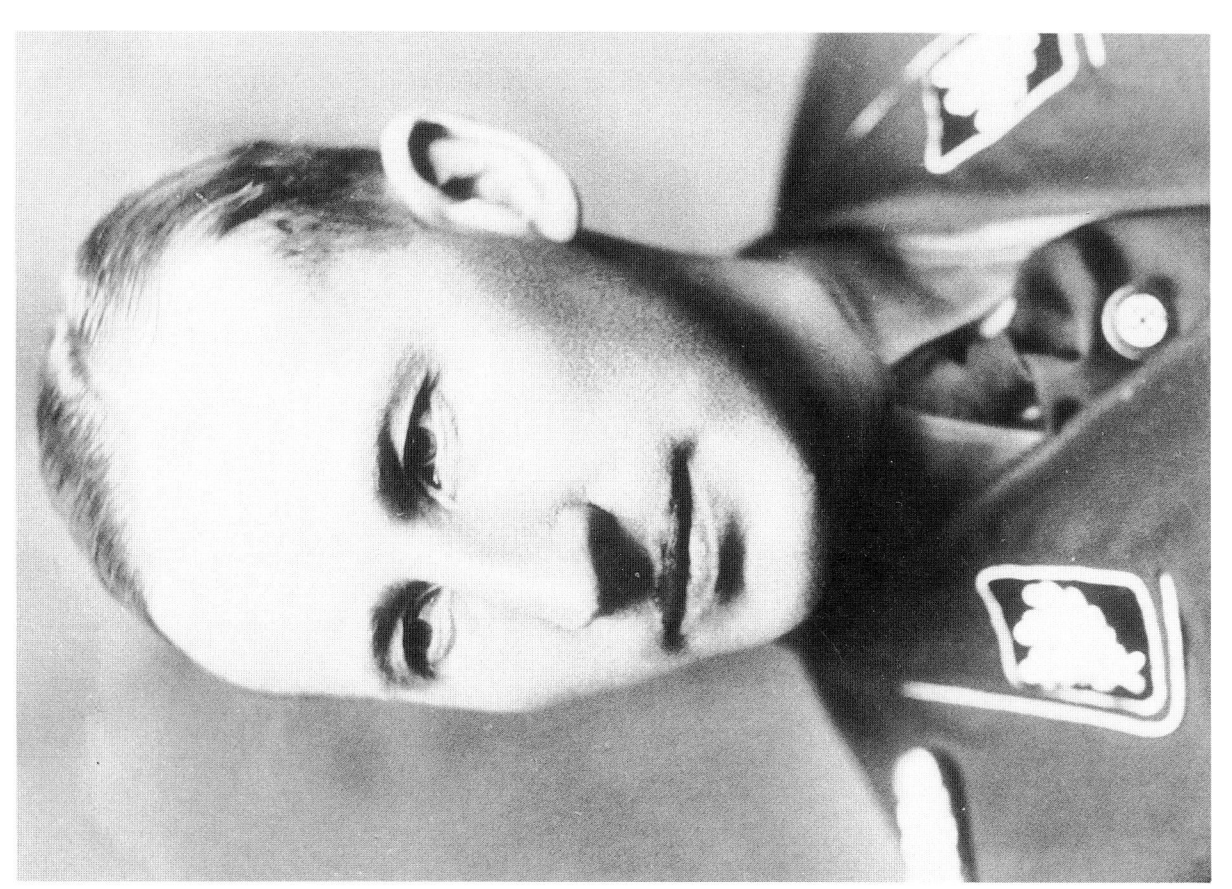

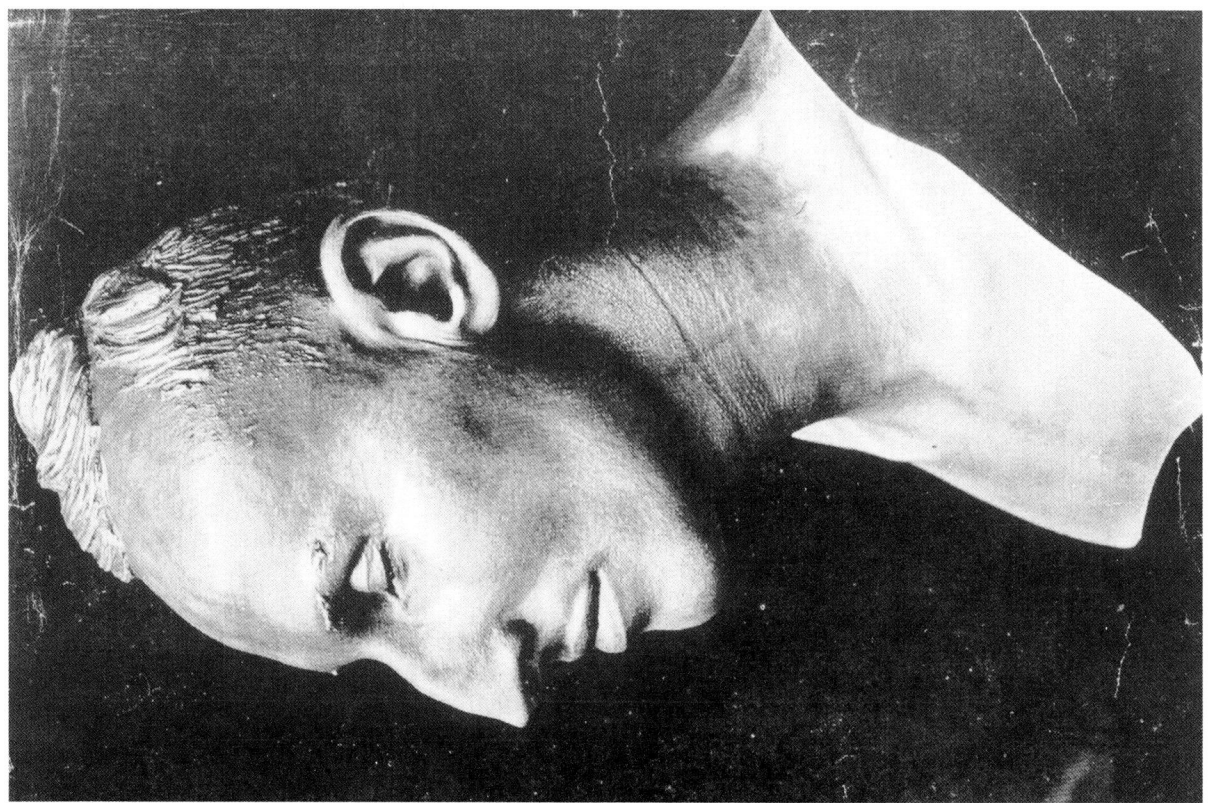

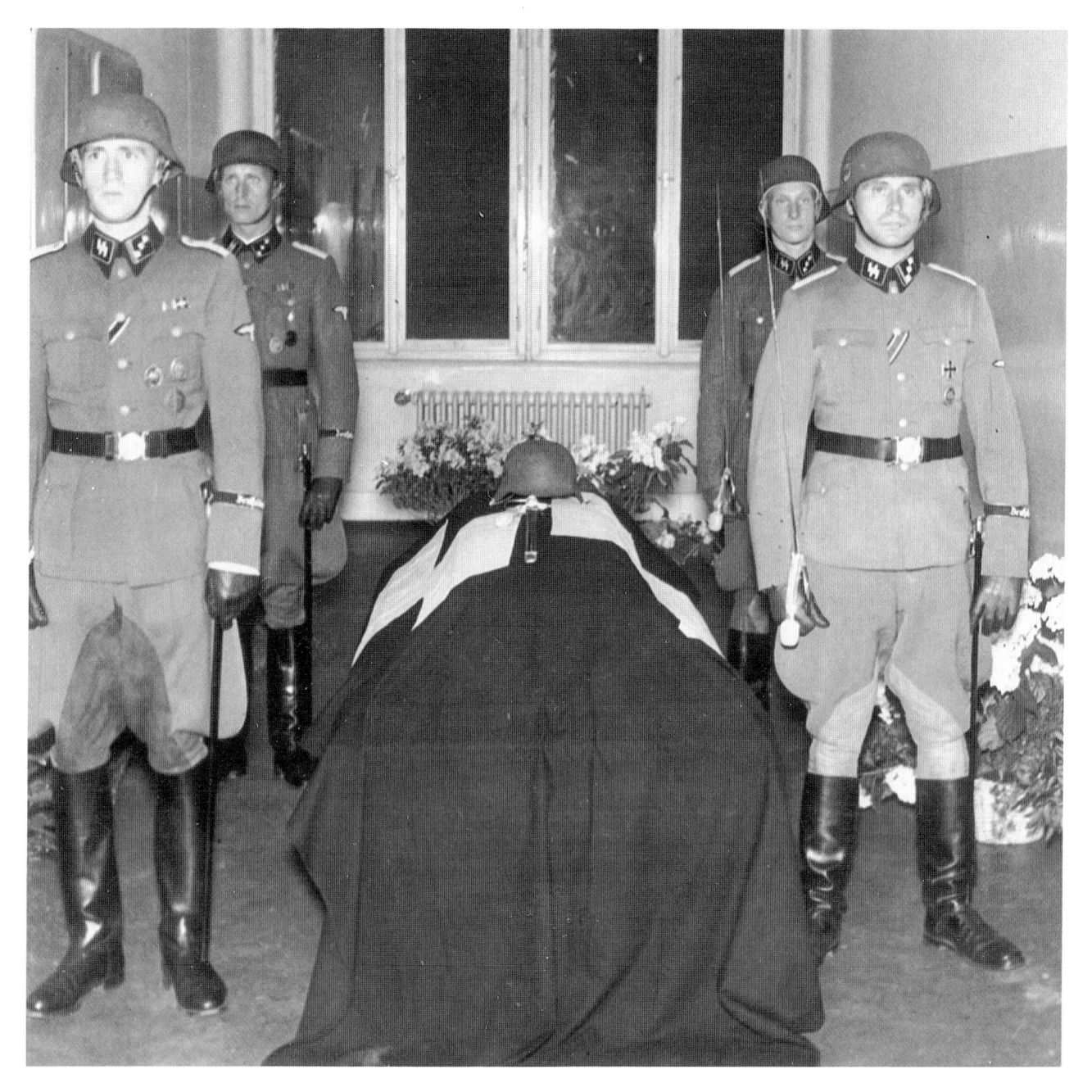

At 04:30 in the morning of 4 June 1942 ⁄⁄-Obergruppenführer Reinhard Heydrich died of infection as a result of his wounds in Praha's Bulovka Hospital. On 6 June his coffin was covered with a ⁄⁄ flag, his helmet and sword and surrounded by a ⁄⁄ Guard of Honor.

tually gotten much worse. In great pain and with a very high temperature, even experimental sulphanomide drugs failed to check Heydrich's blood poisoning. At 04:30 on 04 June 1942 Reinhard Heydrich died, at the age of 38.

An autopsy was ordered and after it was performed a joint report was issued by Professor Hamperl of the German Institute of Pathology and Professor Weyrich of the German Institute of Forensic Medicine. Their conclusion was that the cause of death was blood poisoning (septicaemia) and they further stated: "Death occurred as a consequence of lesions in the vital parenchymatous organs caused by bacteria and possibly poisons carried into them by bomb splinters and deposited chiefly in the pleura, the diaphragm and tissues near the spleen, there agglomerating and multiplying."

With Heydrich's death in the early morning hours of 04 June the focus of German attention shifted

A ⚡⚡ Honor Guard detachment accompanied Heydrich's body from Bulovka Hospital to a waiting artillery caisson and then on to Hradčany Castle overlooking Praha.

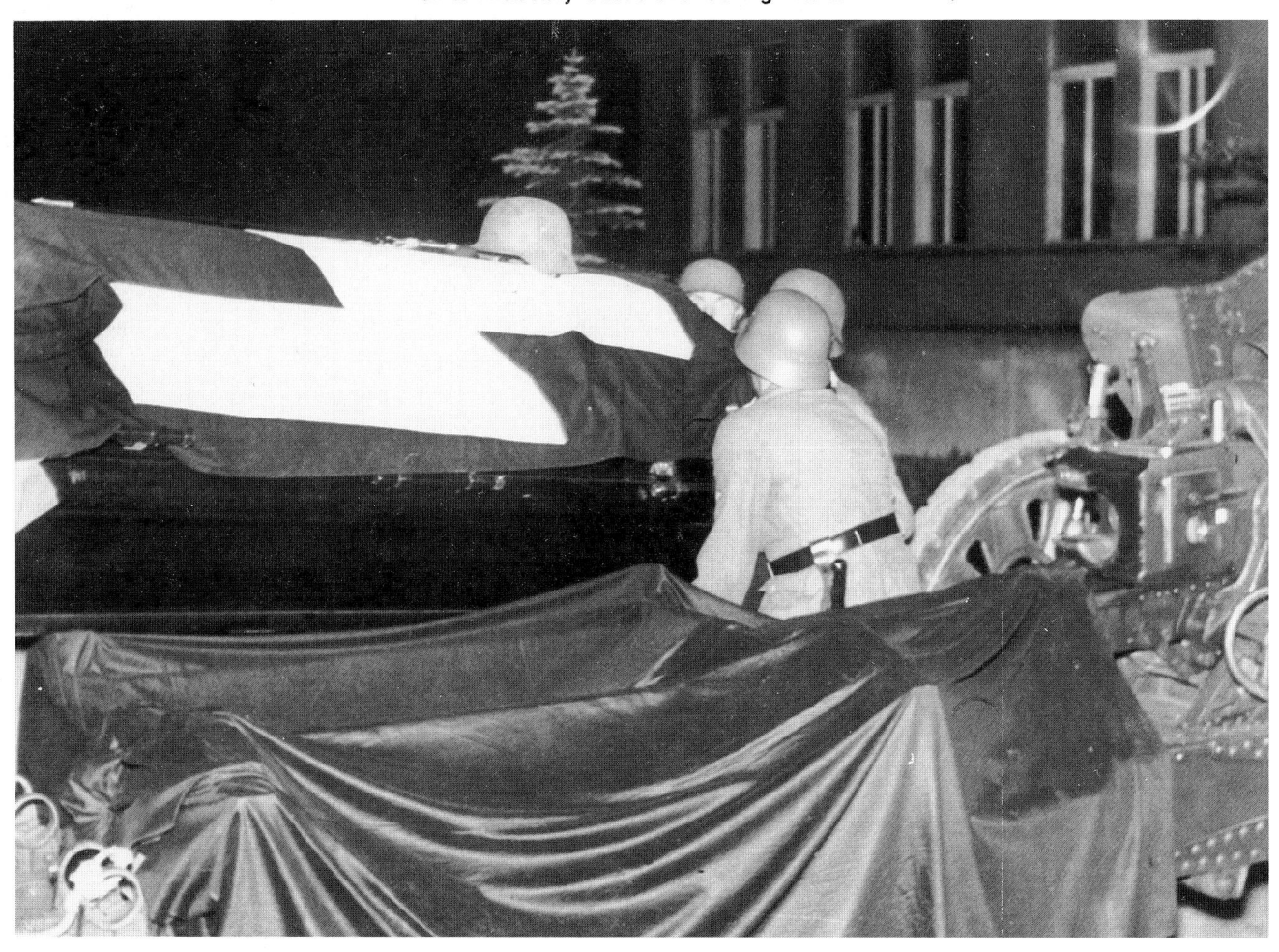

Reinhard Heydrich's body left Bulovka Hospital in a dramatic torch-lit ceremony at midnight 6 June 1942 to the sound of drums.

briefly from the search for Heydrich's attackers to the pageantry of the ceremonial funeral of one of their most respected and capable colleagues. On 06 June Heydrich's body was placed in a coffin covered by a ⚡⚡ flag topped with his helmet and sword. A helmeted honor guard of four ⚡⚡ officers stood along side the coffin with swords drawn.

At midnight on the 6th pallbearers moved the body to a waiting artillery caisson in the hospital yard. Accompanied by the music of pipes and drums the coffin was moved to a specially prepared flower-lined plinth at the Matyášuv Gate outside Hradčany Castle. Below a huge Iron Cross and between monumental torches an eight-man ⚡⚡ honor guard stood watch as the day-long funeral ceremony began.

Himmler paid his respects as did many of Heydrich's ⚡⚡ colleagues, officials of the Protektorate government and thousands of citizens of Praha. An oration praising Heydrich was delivered by his replacement, ⚡⚡-Obergruppenführer and new Reichsprotektor of Bohemia and Moravia, Kurt Daluege. At 18:00 a formation of aircraft flew low overhead as the honor guard fired a salute, signaling the end of the ceremony. The coffin was loaded on a gun carriage pulled by a halftrack which slowly wound its way down Nerudova Street, over the Karl's Bridge, up the Vltava Quay to Narodni Street and then over Wenceslas Square to Hlavni railway station. At 20:45 the special train carrying Heydrich's remains left Praha for Berlin.

The Berlin funeral ceremony for Reinhard Heydrich on 09 June was the grandest of any funeral ceremony conducted during the Third Reich. It was held in the huge (151 feet *[46 m]* x 63 feet *[19 m]*) Mosaic Hall of the new Reichschancellery on Voßstraße, just south of the Brandenburg Gate. The building was only three years old and of magnificent construction. Wall sconces containing live flames lit the 52 feet *(16 m)* high artificially darkened room in which over 1000 were seated.

Heydrich's body lay in state outside the Matyášuv Gate in the Hradčany Castle complex in Praha.

Reichsführer-SS Heinrich Himmler accompanied Heydrich's boys to pay their last respects to their father at Hradčany Castle in Praha.

Hitler himself delivered the funeral oration: "I will devote only a few words to the dead. He was one of the best of all National Socialists, one of the staunchest defenders of the idea of the German Reich and one of the greatest adversaries of all of the enemies of that Reich. He has fallen as a

From Praha's Hradčany Castle Heydrich's remains began their journey home to Germany.

martyr to the cause of the preservation and security of the Reich. As Führer of the party and Führer of the German Reich, I award you my dear comrade Heydrich, after our comrade Todt, the greatest distinction I can confer: the highest decoration of the German Order."

Following the ceremony the coffin was transported through the streets of Berlin on a gun carriage towed by a halftrack to a simple grave in Invaliden cemetery.

Heydrich's boys stood with Heinrich Himmler (just ahead of their mother, Lina von Osten Heydrich) as their father's coffin was removed from Hradčany Castle for its journey to Berlin. At 18:00 while a formation of aircraft flew overhead and a salute was fired nearby, Heydrich's coffin was loaded on a gun carriage pulled by a halftrack for the trip through the streets of Praha to Hlavni railway station At 20:45 the train carrying Heydrich's body departed for Berlin. His stay in Praha had lasted just eight months.

On 09 June 1942 Heydrich's flag draped coffin was carried atop a gun carriage through the streets of Berlin on its way to *Invaliden Cemetery* where he was buried.

Adolf Hitler at the funeral ceremony for Reinhard Heydrich in Berlin.

A commemorative postage stamp featuring the death mask of Reinhard Heydrich was issued in 1943 by the German Government for Bohemia and Moravia (Böhmen und Mähren) on the first anniversary of his death. The death mask shown on the stamp was the work of Berlin sculptor Professor Rotter. Shown here at 2 x the actual size.

Adolf Hitler paid his last respects to SS-Obergruppenführer Reinhard Heydrich. Below, the *Vltava Quay* in Praha was renamed *Reinhard Heydrich Ufer* in 1943.

DESTRUCTION OF LIDICE

Back in the Protektorate of Bohemia and Moravia the Gestapo had made very little progress in locating the well-hidden assassins of Heydrich. They were using every available means from torture to execution to try to turn up a lead, but nobody was talking.

For some time information had been turned up among captured paratroopers, their possessions or acquaintances which had implicated the families Horák and Stříbrný (both of whom had sons in the RAF in England) living in the small town of Lidice, near Kladno, about ten miles northwest of Praha. The village had been surrounded by the Gestapo and carefully searched on 28 May. It was searched for a second time on 04 June and all of the members of the Horák and Stříbrný families were arrested. No evidence of complicity in the attack on Reinhard Heydrich was to be found.

Finally, as Heydrich was being buried, Adolf Hitler announced he would be patient no longer and ordered the complete obliteration of the little Bohemian village of Lidice as partial vengeance for the assassination of Heydrich. Karl Frank phoned SD Chief Böhme in Praha and instructed him to carry out the previously planned destruction.

By 22:00 on 09 June Gestapo agents from Praha were joined in Kladno by two companies of police in battle-dress, and a squad of security police under ⁄⁄-Hauptsturmführer Max Rostock, which would handle executions. By truck, bus and by car they drove the remaining one and a half miles to Lidice, which was quickly surrounded.

The Gestapo set up a command post in the orchard adjacent to the Horák family barn, from

Motion picture and still photographers recorded details of the preparations for and the destruction of the small Czech town of Lidice.

German army clerks at Lidice make an accounting of the identity and belongings of the victims. Below, a scene of the destruction of Lidice.

SS-Obergruppenführer Karl Hermann Frank *(L)* greets *SS*-Obergruppenführer Kurt Daluege *(R)* who succeeded Reinhard Heydrich as Deputy Reichsprotektor of Bohemia and Moravia on 18 June 1942. Frank was hung near Praha on 22 May 1946 and Daluege was hung on 24 October 1946 after they were sentenced to death by Czechoslovakian courts.

which they sent out teams of agents and police to bring in the residents from every house in the village. The mayor was required to deliver the village register to the Gestapo and as the townspeople were brought to the orchard they were checked against it. Women and children were taken to the village school and the men over 16 years of age were locked up in the barn and cellar on the Horák farm. Trucks moved from house to house collecting everything of value in preparation of the destruction of the town.

At 07:00 on 10 June *SS*-Obergruppenführer Karl Frank arrived in Lidice from Praha to observe the progress of his troops. Many buildings within the town were already burning when the first group of ten men were lined up in front of mattresses leaning against Horák's barn, and shot. As additional groups of ten men were brought to the execution ground the women and children were loaded in busses and trucks and taken to the elementary school in Kladno for processing. By noon, 173 men of Lidice had been executed. Eleven other

The 173 men of Lidice were assembled alongside a building on the Horák farm and shot on 10 June 1942. The mattresses along the wall were apparently intended to prevent ricocheting bullets.

men of Lidice who were working away from the village at the time, were later captured and executed in Praha along with the Horák and Stříbrný families.

In Kladno the division of the remnants of the Lidice families was carried out over two days. 185 women were selected for immediate transfer to Ravensbrück concentration camp north of Berlin. Four pregnant women were taken to Praha where they gave birth to their babies prior to being sent to Ravensbrück. Seven women with infants were first sent to the concentration camp at Terezín and later on to Ravensbrück without their children.

All 108 children of Lidice were processed and deported to Germany for adoption or labor.

On 11 June trucks carrying 30 Jews from Terezín concentration camp arrived in Lidice and began the digging of a common grave for those executed the day before. By nightfall of the 12th the men of Lidice had been buried and the *Reichsarbeitsdienst* (Reich Labor Service) began blowing up the remaining structures in town. Nearly a year later German labor units were still at the site, diverting old roads and a creek and trying to obliterate any possible trace of the town that had been Lidice.

BETRAYAL BY KAREL ČURDA

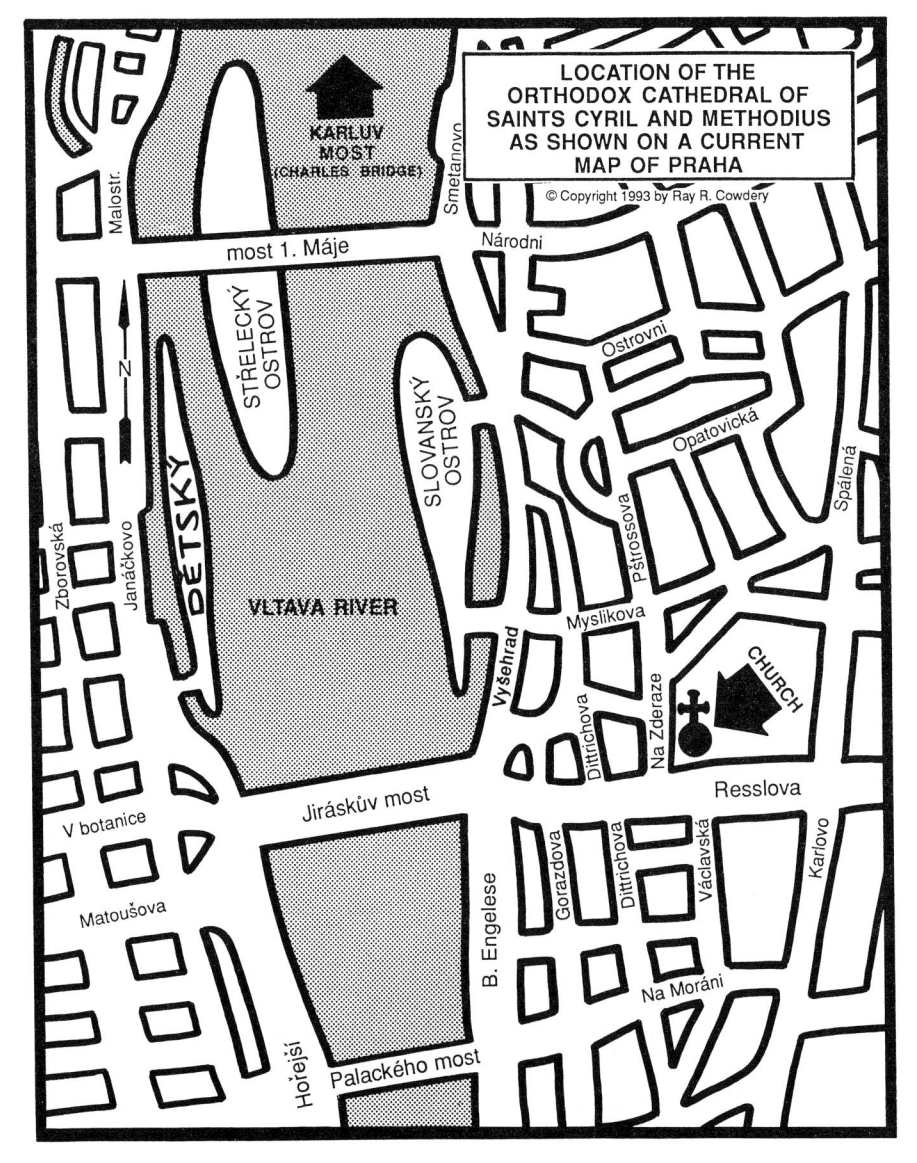

Gabčík, Kubiš and five other Czechoslovakian parachutists had hidden in the crypt of the Orthodox Cathedral of Saints Cyril and Methodius (the Germans called it St. Karl Boromeo Church) on Resslova Street since the 1st of June with only minimal knowledge of what was taking place outside their sanctuary.

Immediately after the attack on Reinhard Heydrich on 27 May, SS-Sturmführer Heinz von Pannwitz, anti-sabotage officer of the Praha Gestapo, had been put in charge of a special investigative section looking into the matter. A well trained and experienced professional policeman, Von Pannwitz was shocked by the counter-productive reprisals taking place in the Protektorate which he felt were preventing people with information from coming forward. Furthermore, he was aware that if a break in the case didn't come soon his superiors would take measures that were far more severe.

Based on information from his investigators Von Pannwitz concluded that fear of reprisals was

This photo of the south side of the Karel Boromejsky Church (now called the Orthodox Cathedral of Saints Cyril and Methodius) was taken by a German photographer looking north along Václavská Street early in the morning of 18 June 1942. The photo at the right below was taken from about the same spot on 30 December 1993. The memorial shown below left, is now attached to the wall of the church above the ventilator opening. It pays tribute to the heroic parachutists and the heroic clergy that sheltered them for a while from German occupation forces.

Water (above) and smoke (below) were both pumped into the crypt beneath the church in an effort to dislodge the parachutists.

Fire hoses pumping 800 gallons per minute were placed through a ventilator in the side of the church in an effort to flood the basement crypt where parachutists were hiding. Below, ventilator opening indicated by arrow.

The Germans took this picture of Dr. Vladimír Petřek, priest of the Orthodox Cathedral of Saints Cyril and Methodius.

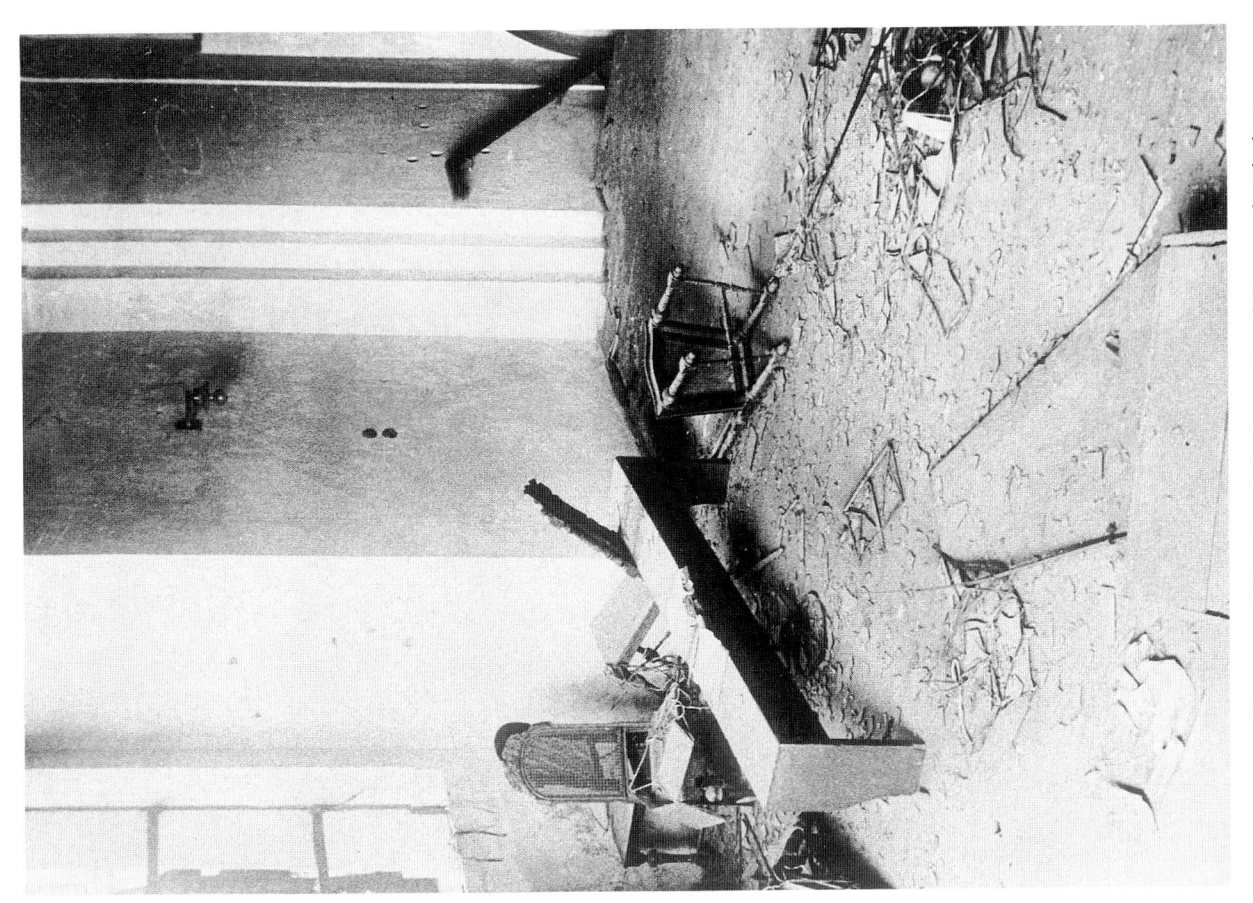

The west-end balcony of the church in the wake of the gun battle between the parachutists and the Germans.

preventing people with valuable leads from coming forward with them. Building a solid case for his point of view Von Pannwitz went to Karl Frank with an amnesty proposal which would provide refuge and safety for anyone informing on or giving information which would lead to the capture of Heydrich's assassins. Much to Von Pannwitzs" surprise, Frank ordered the broadcast of the amnesty on 13 June 1942 while the dust was still settling on the village of Lidice.

The amnesty announcement was a great success by any measure, eliciting tips for the police from more than 1800 citizens. Naturally, many letters to the authorities contained false clues intended to mislead the Gestapo and buy time for the parachutists. One anonymous letter mailed to the Czechoslovakian police in Benesov however, had a message that could not be overlooked. The writer confessed that fear and anxiety about continuing reprisals against innocent Czechoslovakians had caused him to write. He stated flatly that it was Jan Kubiš and Josef Gabčík that had killed Reinhard Heydrich, and that it was useless for the police to look any further.

Still, this single letter could not put an end to the matter. Gabčík and Kubiš were nowhere to be found and could not even be questioned regarding the assassination. On 15 June Frank was informed by Reichsführer-SS Heinrich Himmler that Hitler had ordered the execution of up to 30,000 Czechoslovakians in retaliation for the killing of Heydrich.

The man who had written the anonymous letter to the Benesov police could take no more. Sergeant Karel Čurda, OUT DISTANCE parachutist and SOE operative decided to go the the Gestapo. On 16 June he voluntarily walked into the Gestapo Headquarters in Peček Palace in central Praha to surrender. Čurda's Gestapo interrogators soon established that he had been SOE trained in Britain and knew far more than he had at first admitted. He was quickly searched and the Gestapo found his SOE-issued cyanide capsule. Very intensive interrogation followed during which Čurda stated that he had become disillusioned with the Beneš government-in-exile in England and wished to save himself and his family from further harm.

The crypt beneath the Orthodox Cathedral of Saints Cyril and Methodius where the parachutists sought safety and died. The piles of human bones on the floor were removed from the niches above by the parachutists so they would have a protected place to lie down and sleep.

The restored nave and altar of the Orthodox Cathedral of Saints Cyril and Methodius as it looks today.

This balcony railing is still full of bullet holes over 50 years after the battle occurred. See page 103.

Karl Frank paces as the German police bring in prisoners in an attempt to identify bodies.

Pointing to the dead parachutist is Chief of the *Gestapo Investigative Commission,* ᛋᛋ-Sturmführer Heinz von Pannwitz.

Karl Frank bends over the corpse of one of the parachutists as the Czech traitor Karel Čurda (arrow) makes an identification. A horde of German policemen look on.

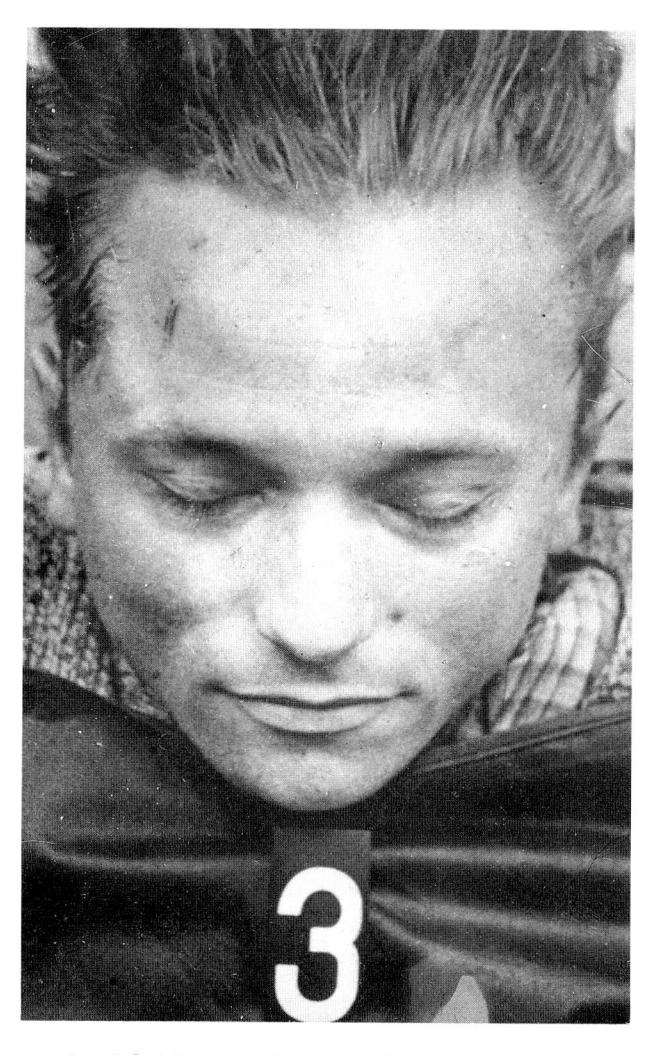

Josef Gabčík who aimed the Sten gun at Heydrich, killed himself in the crypt of the church with his last bullet.

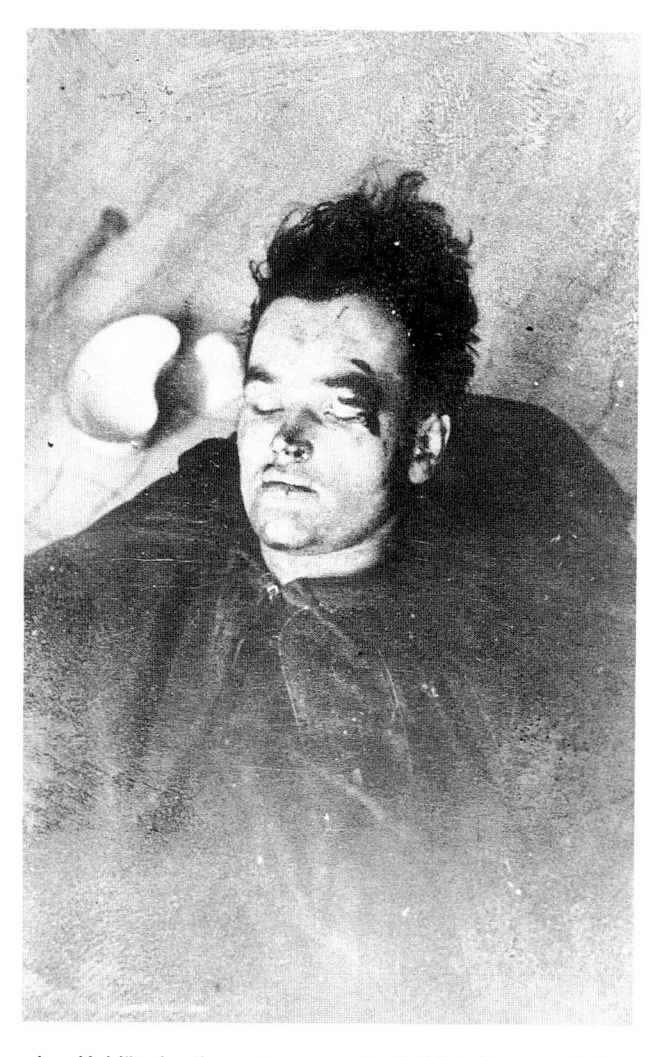

Jan Kubiš who threw the grenade that fatally wounded Reinhard Heydrich, died in the hospital after being wounded on the church balcony.

As Čurda told all that he knew, Von Pannwitz began to direct his agents in a round-up of everyone mentioned in the interrogation. It was soon clear that the third-floor apartment of the Moravec family on Biskupova Street in the suburb of Zizkov was near the center of the underground web.

At 05:00 on the 17th German police broke down the door of the Moravec home and dragged the three occupants from their beds. "Aunt Marie" excused herself to use the toilet, locked herself in and ingested the cyanide in her suicide capsule. Furious at losing one of the conspirators the Gestapo dragged Ata Moravec and his father from the building. As the Gestapo closed in on the home of underground leader Jan Zelenka (HAJASKY) just down the street, he quietly bit into his cyanide capsule making certain the Germans would get no information from him. The Moravecs were repeatedly searched and finally lodged in the cells beneath Peček Palace for further questioning.

Late the same day, 21 year old Ata Moravec was beginning to show signs of weakening under intensive, non-stop torture and interrogation. In a last desperate effort to get him to talk two Germans brought him his mothers severed head floating in a tub of water. Crying hysterically, Ata Moravec told the Gestapo that his mother had instructed him to take refuge in the Orthodox Cathedral of Saints Cyril and Methodius if he was ever desperate for shelter.

Vojtěch Lukaštik was killed in a shoot out with Gestapo agents. The scene was restaged a few minutes later for a German cameraman.

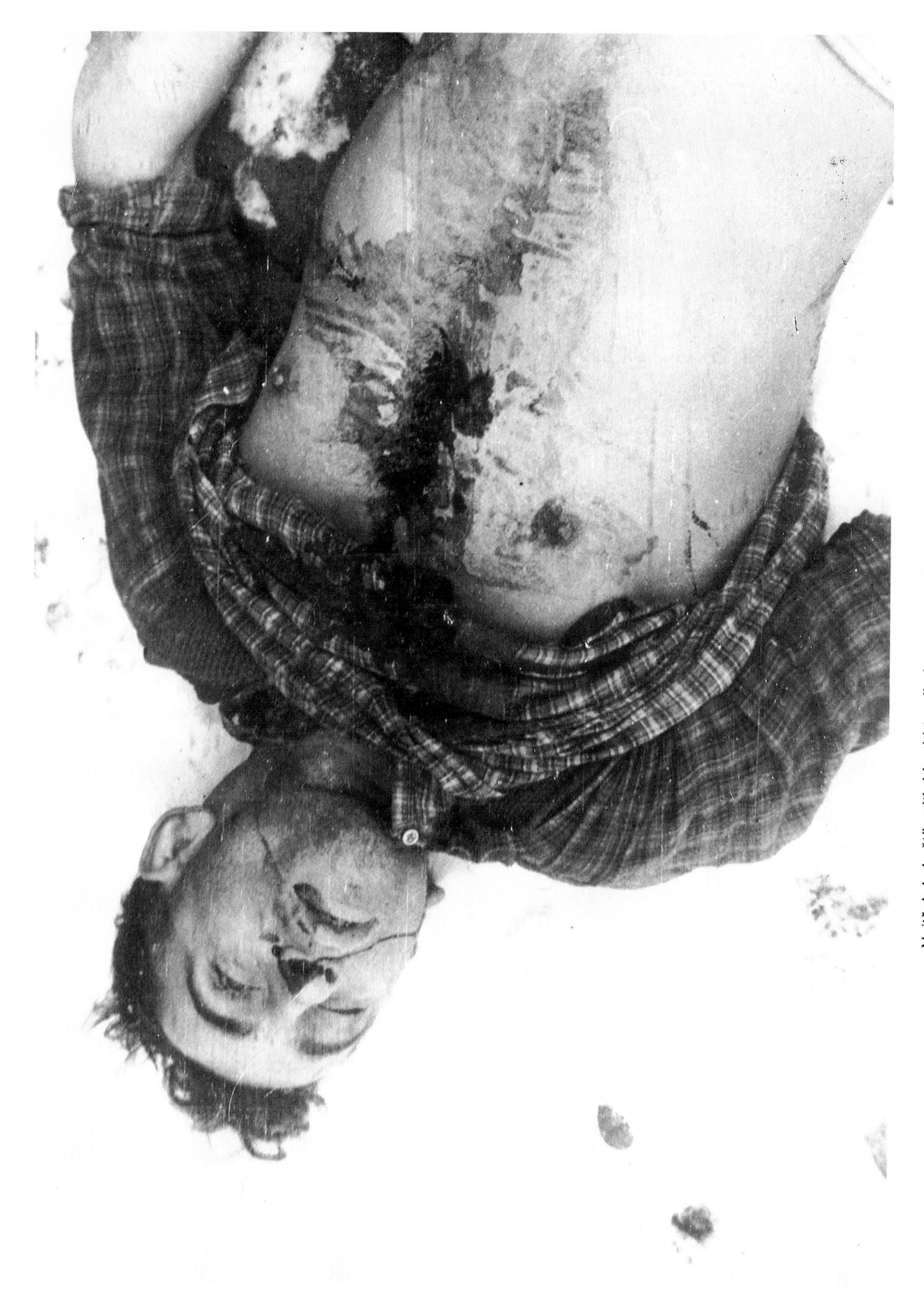

Vojtěch Lukaštík with his shirt pulled up to reveal some of his wounds.

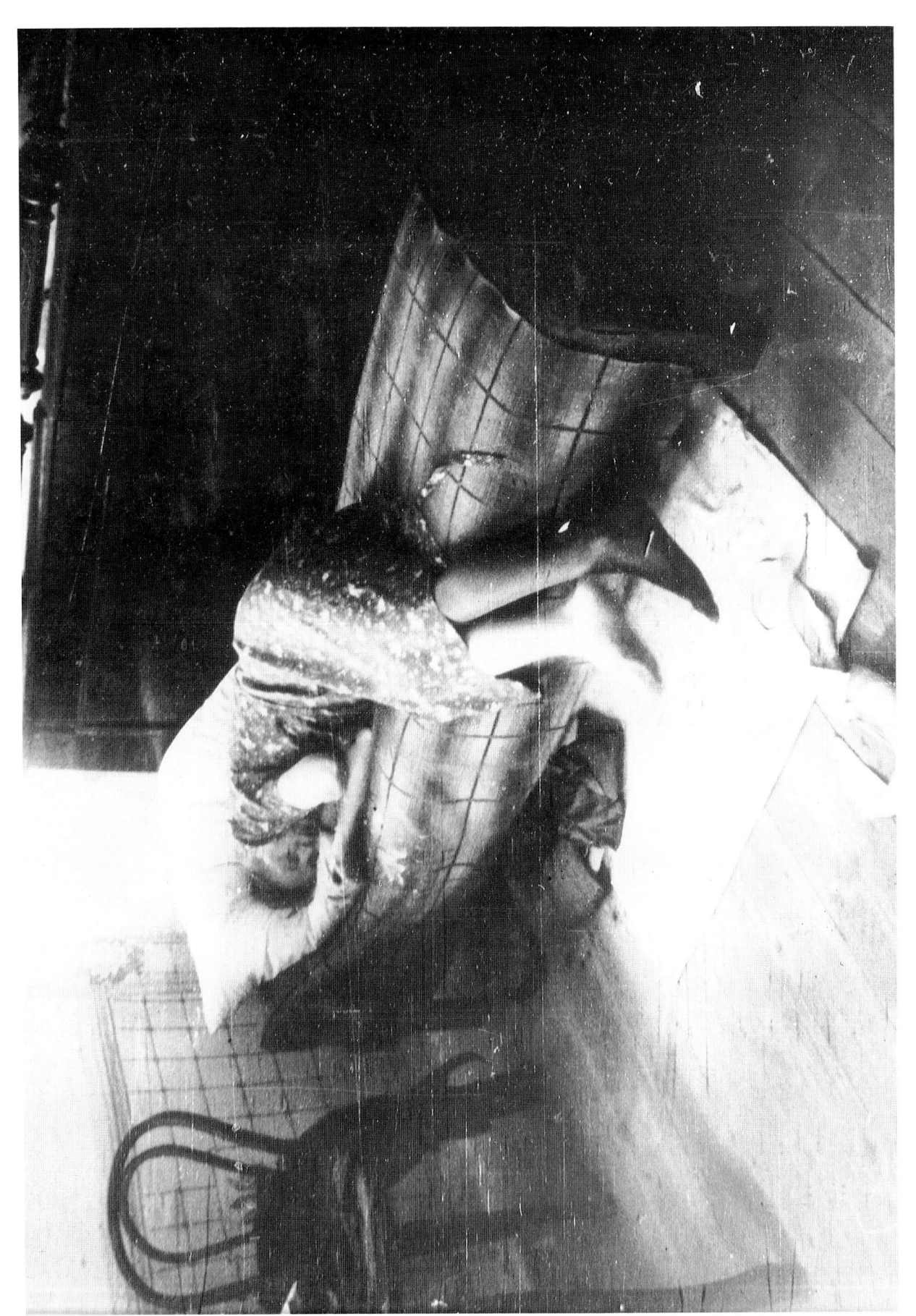

Mrs Moravec, who had helped the parachutists, poisoned herself rather than allowing the Gestapo to take her alive.

THE BATTLE IN THE CHURCH

Seizing on Ata Moravec's small clue Von Pannwitz and his staff sprang into action. At midnight Karl Frank was informed of the break in the case. Unable to locate complete plans for the church it was decided to place two rings of troops around the church to isolate it and to make it less likely that anyone inside could escape into the sewer system and elude authorities by coming to the surface some blocks away. The double cordon of Waffen-SS troops was in place by 03:45 as the sky began to lighten on 18 June 1942. At 04:10 SS-Brigadeführer Karl von Truenfeldt's assault troops in full battle gear passed through the cordon and the zone around the church was closed. SS-Sturmführer Heinz von Pannwitz arrived at the church with his Czechoslovakian interpreter, Josef Chalapsky, and his personal staff at 04:25.

After ringing the night bell Gestapo agents followed by Von Pannwitz were let into the church by the janitor and immediately began a sweep of the main floor. They were carefully observed by Opálka, Kubiš and Švarc who were standing guard while the other parachutists slept in the crypt below. As the Gestapo approached the altar the three parachutists waiting on the balcony opened fire, wounding one German.

In response to the shots being fired inside, the troops outside the church opened fire on the church windows endangering the Gestapo agents inside. Von Pannwitz quickly withdrew his agents and turned the problem over to the Waffen-SS commander and his assault troops, asking them to try to capture the parachutists alive.

Von Truenfeldt ordered his heavily armed men into the church where they immediately began an assault on the choir loft where Opálka, Kubiš and Švarc were taking cover. When the violence ended just before 07:00 the nave of the church was in shambles. Two of the parachutists were found dead and Kubiš, unconscious, had only minutes to live. Von Pannwitz was furious that the three had been killed as he felt it would have been easy to kill them hours earlier if that had been the objective.

In the meantime, the church Priest Dr Petřek, had been interrogated and admitted that there were other parachutists in the crypt. He was forced to show the Germans the small entrance to the

Morgue photos of Jaroslav Švarc *(L)* and Adolf Opálka *(R)*.

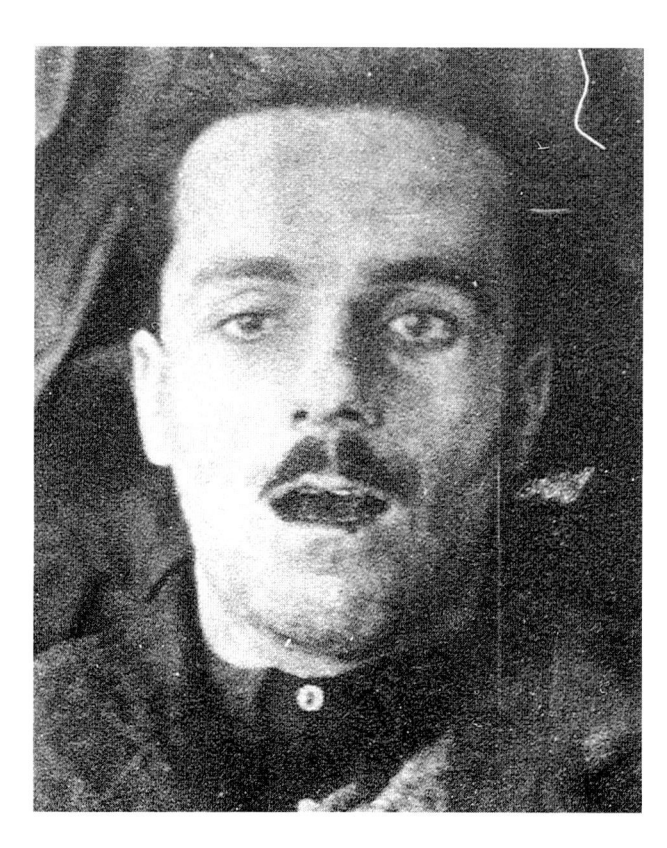

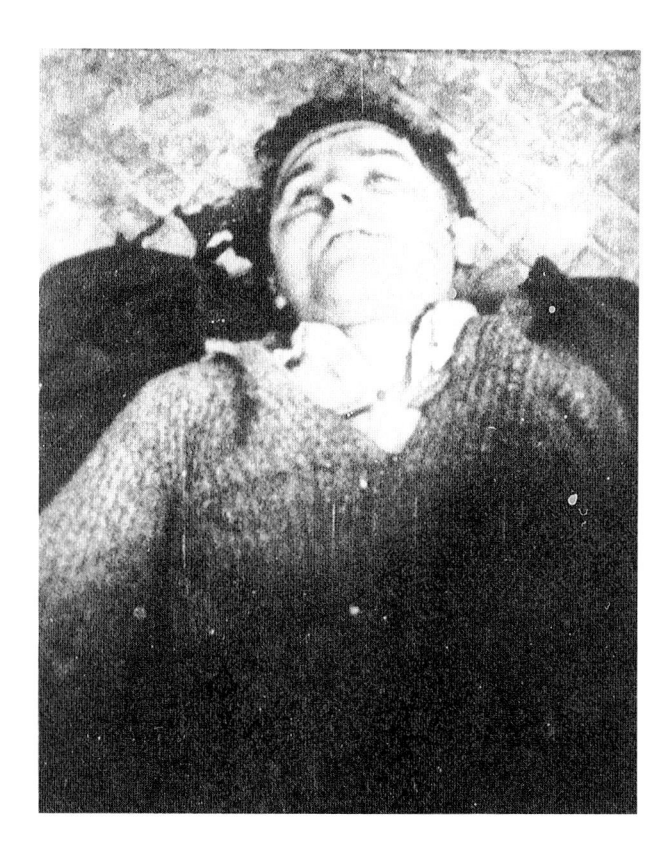

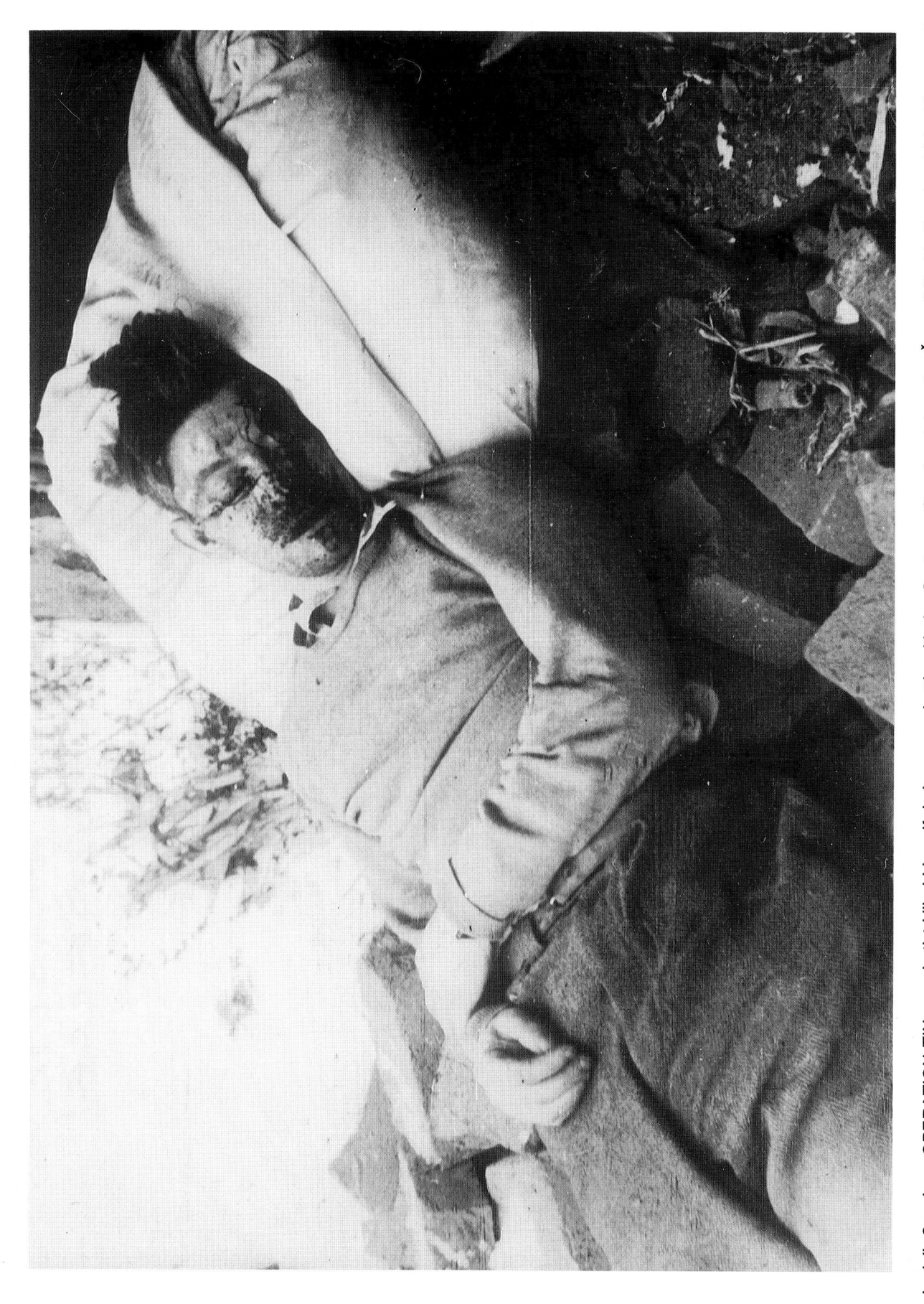

Ludvik Cupal, an OPERATION TIN parachutist killed himself during a gun battle with the Gestapo. Cupal and Jaroslav Švarc (killed in the church) had been sent to Czechoslovakia to kill a German collaborator.

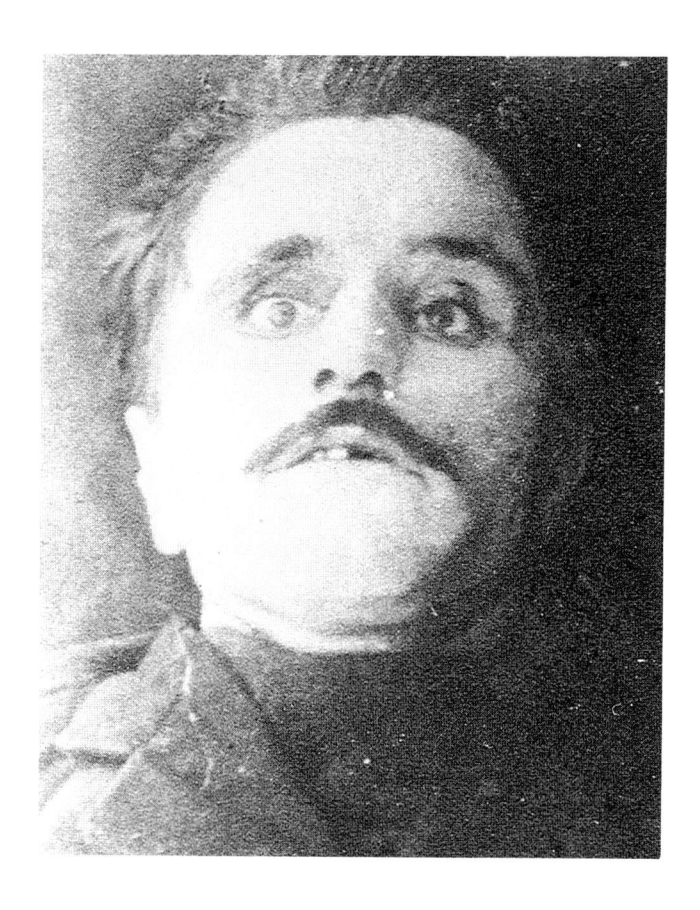

Morgue photos of Jan Hrubý *(above)*, Josef Bublík *(L)* and Josef Valčík*(R)*.

crypt, a thick stone slab hidden beneath a carpet near the front of the church. Von Pannwitz decided to try to "talk" the remaining four parachutists out of the crypt alive. Petřek and Čurda were brought to the ventilation shaft on the outside of the the church where they shouted to the men hiding below, asking them to surrender. The suggestion was answered by a volley of shots from the crypt.

By then the Praha fire department had arrived on the scene with instructions to flood the crypt with water in order to force the surrender of the four men inside. The grill was ripped from the ventilation shaft on the outside the church and tear gas grenades were thrown in. The parachutists responded by tossing them back out on the street. Finally, the fire department was ready and a hose was placed in the ventilator opening to flood the crypt. Below, the parachutists used a ladder to eject the hose. On the street firemen grabbed the ladder, pulling it from the opening and resuming the flooding process.

As time wore on it became clear that the water in the crypt was rising very slowly as much of it seeped away through floor drains and cracks in the building. Karl Frank was growing more anxious that the four trapped parachutists would cre-

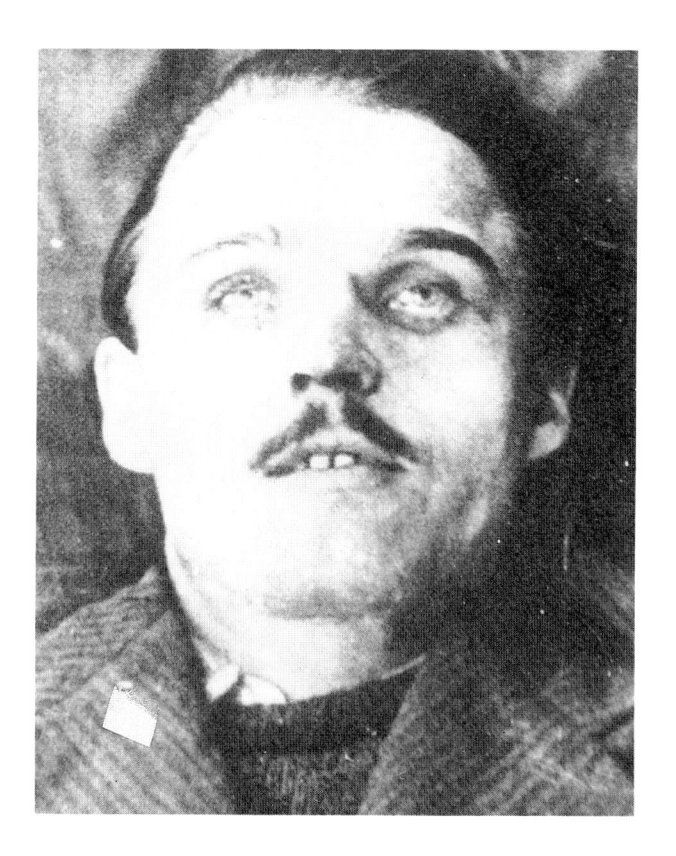

93

After the battle in the church, troops of ǁ-Brigadeführer Karl von Truenfeldt posed for a photo nearby. Over 750 soldiers and an unknown number of German police were involved in the six hour battle, of which 14 were killed and 21 wounded. There were 11 parachutist's weapons found inside the church but not a single round of ammunition.

ate or discover some unknown passage and somehow slip from his grasp. He decided there was no longer time or reason to follow Von Pannwitzs' plan to bring the parachutists out alive.

The first attempt to storm the crypt using the small entrance revealed by Dr Petřek ended in failure with the Waffen-ǁ troops retreating with two wounded. Weary of the conflicting desires of Karl Frank and Heinz von Pannwitz that were putting his troops at risk, Von Truenfeldt ordered his men to use explosives to blow open the larger main entrance to the crypt, located near the altar. When the dust of the explosion cleared and the troops prepared to rush the crypt, four shots rang out followed by perfect silence. The last four parachutists killed themselves to avoid capture. As the bodies were removed from the crypt the Germans found eleven guns, but not a single round of ammunition.

In spite of the death of Reinhard Heydrich's assassins in the church in Praha, the terror was not yet over for the country of Czechoslovakia. On 24 June 1942 the Germans destroyed the village of Ležáky and murdered all its adult inhabitants. Bishop Gorazd and all the other church officials implicated in the shelter of the parachutists were executed in Kobilisi. 252 relatives and friends of the parachutists were executed at Mauthausen concentration camp on 24 October 1942. And thousands of ordinary Czechoslovakians who had nothing to do with the plot against Heydrich were arrested and hundreds of them were executed.

Karel Čurda and Viliam Gerik were each paid five million Czech Crowns of the Heydrich reward and spent the rest of the war in service to the German occupiers. Another five million Crowns was divided among seven Germans and the remaining five million was divided among 53 Czechoslovakians.

From left to right the skulls of Jaroslav Švarc, Adolf Opálka, Josef Bublík, Josef Valčík and Jan Hrubý. The heads of Gabčík and Kubiš were detached and kept preserved in flasks at Gestapo Headquarters in Peček Palace until the end of WWII, when they disappeared.

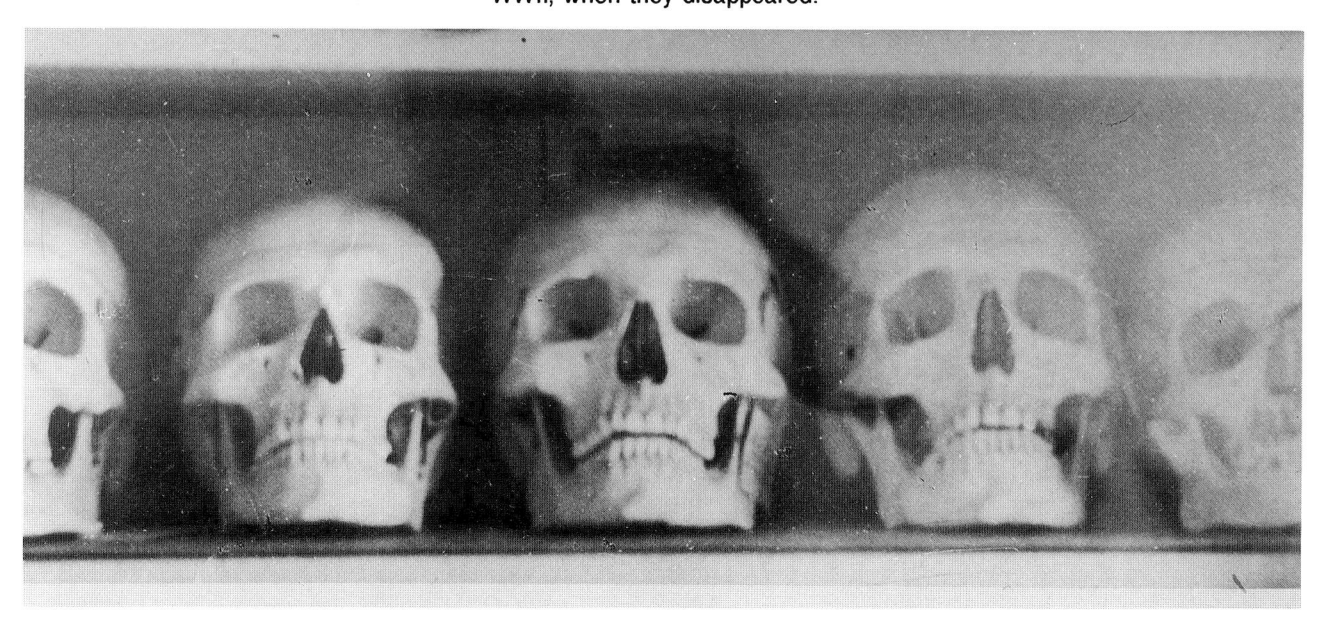

Professor Jaromir Tesar and Police Inspector Miloslav Nečásek study a corpse. Nečásek made photographs of the skulls of the dead parachutists.

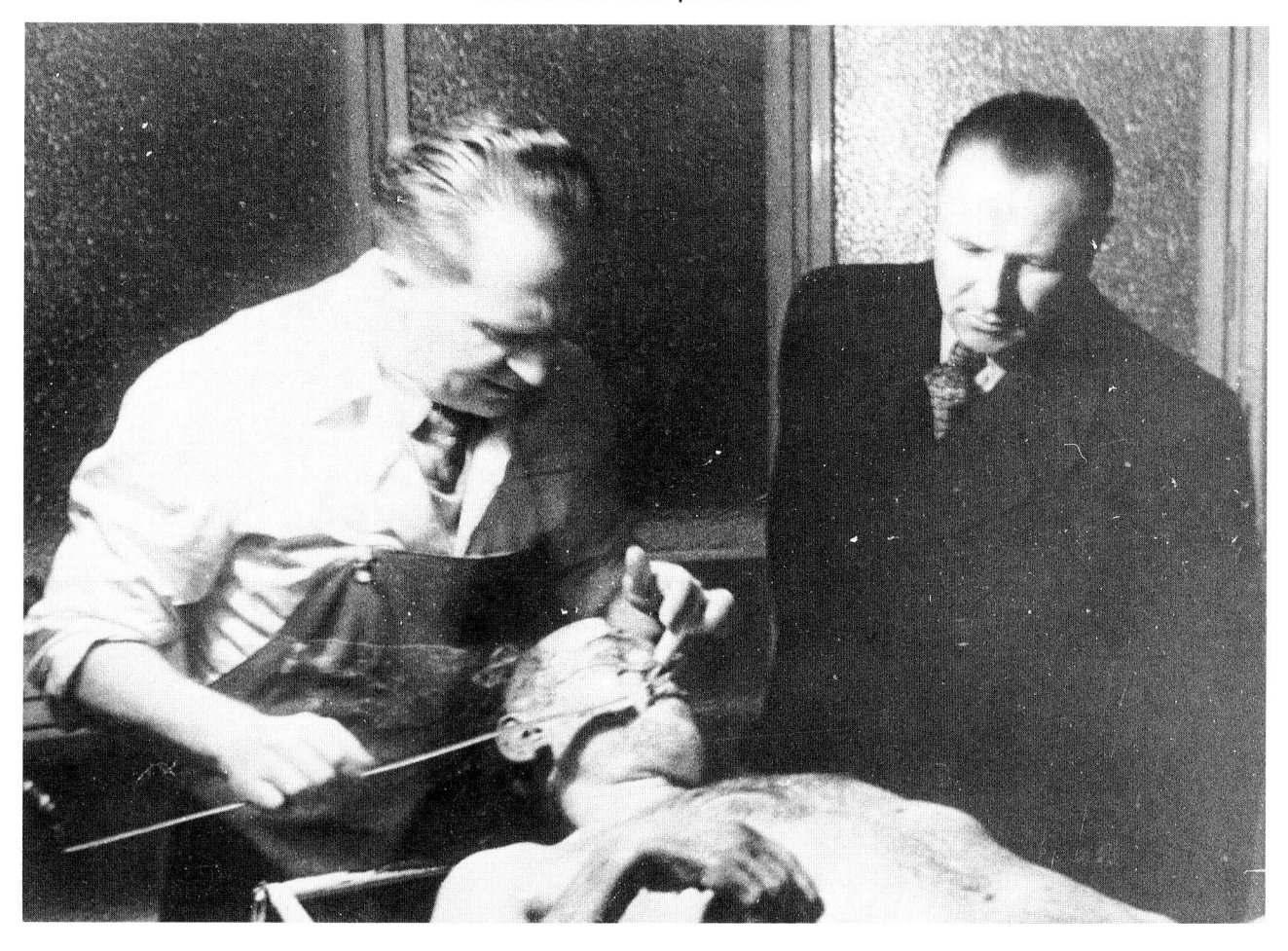

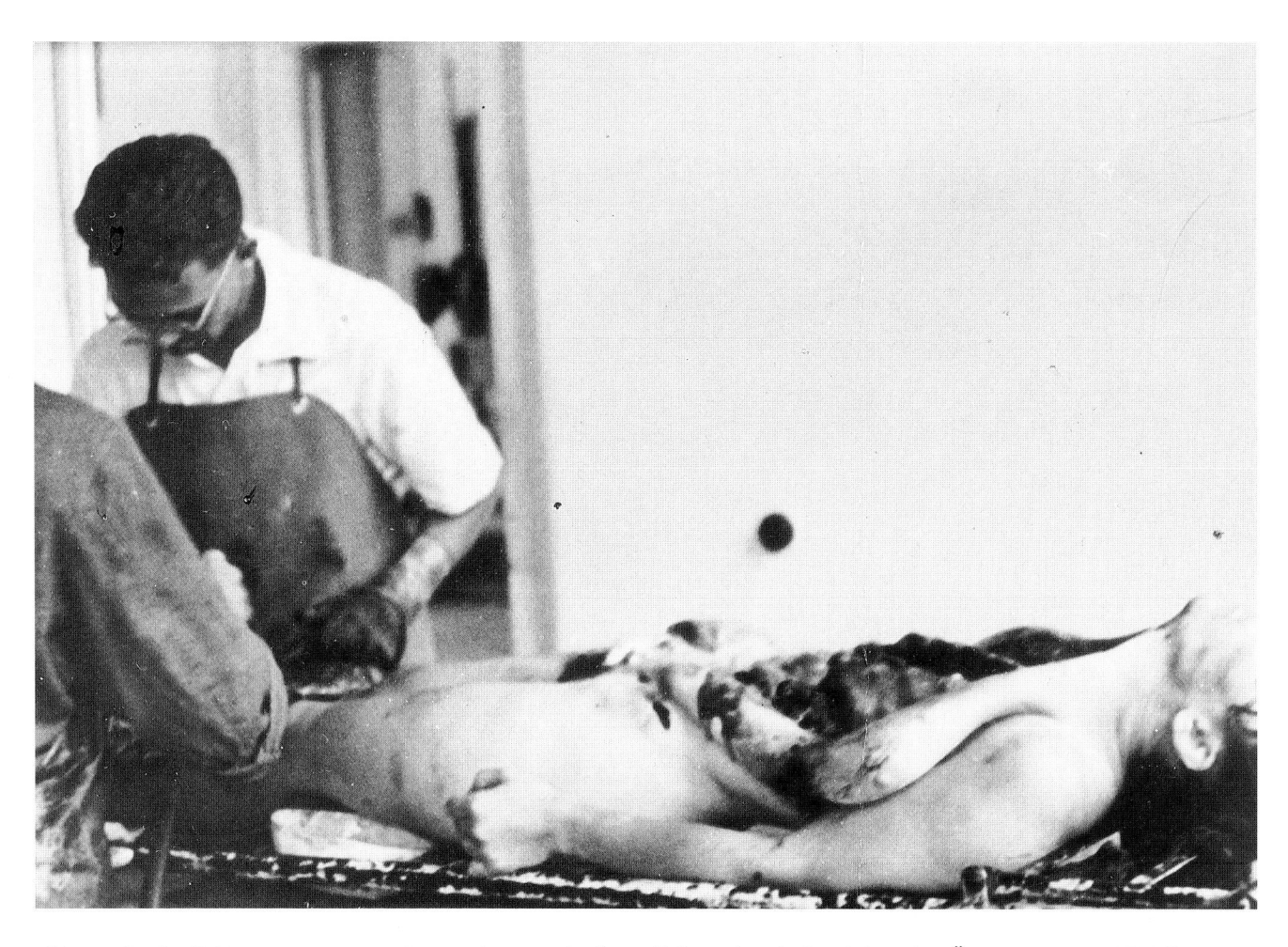

Above, Dr Steffel performed autopsies on the parachutists. Below, the skulls of Jaroslav Švarc and Josef Bublík were saved for clinical study. Each committed suicide by shooting himself in the right temple as can be seen in the photo.

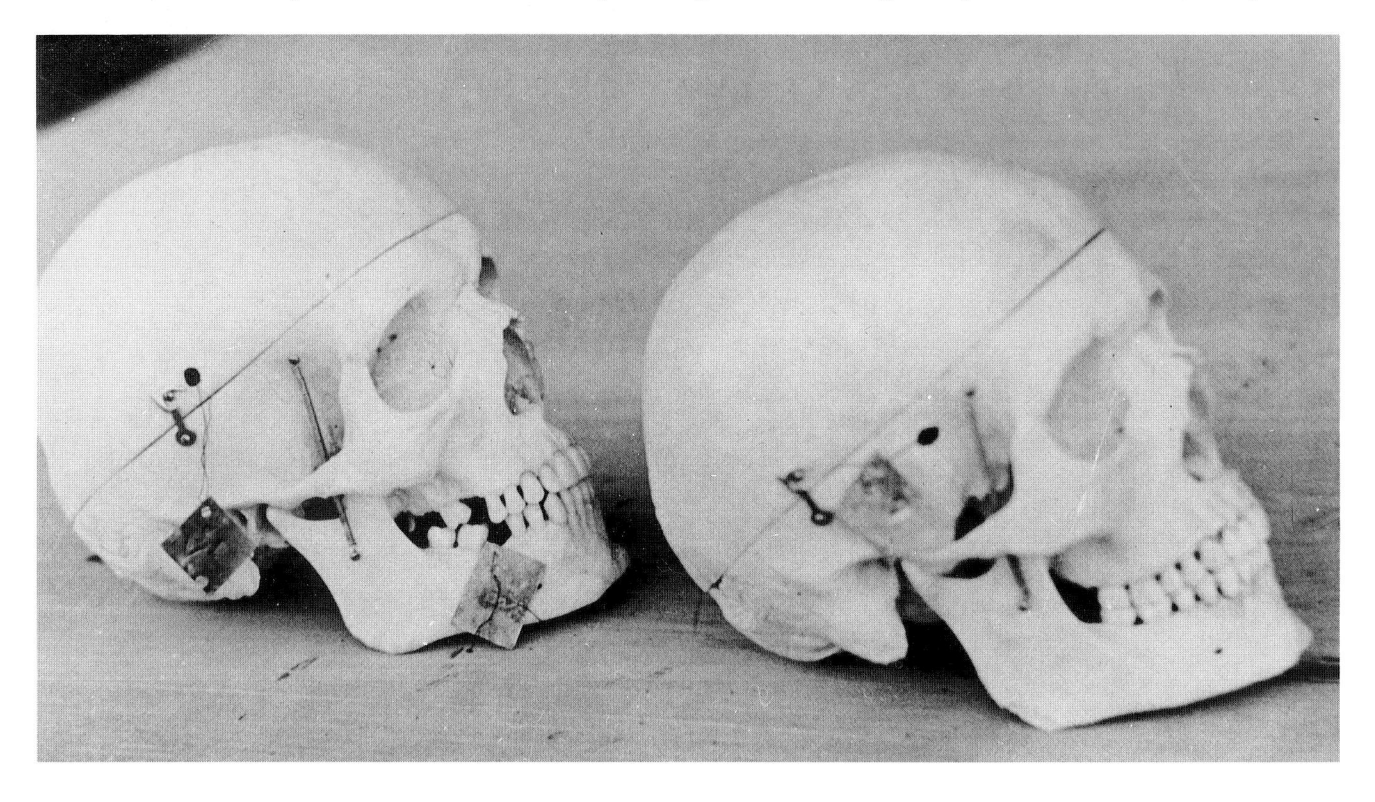

In June 1943 the Germans dedicated this monument to the memory of Reinhard Heydrich at the spot where the assassination attempt had taken place.

Lina Heydrich saluted as Reichsarbeitsdienst platoon I-385 in training at Brno was given the name *"Reinhard Heydrich Platoon"* on 21 September 1942.

At war's end Karl Frank was in US custody in Wiesbaden. He was deported to Praha at the request of Czechoslovakian authorities. Below, Frank was found guilty of his crimes on 21 May 1946.

Kurt Daluege steps to the gallows.

The last seconds of Karl Frank's life.

The traitors Viliam Gerik (shown here) and Karel Čurda were hung on the same day - 29 April 1947.

The last *public* hanging in Praha occurred on 22 May 1946 when Karl Hermann Frank drew his final breath.

Praha today. The Matyášuv gate at Hradčany Castle *(L)*. Compare with photo on page 67. Praha's Old Town Square *(R)*. Compare with photo on page 24. The beautifully restored Černinsky Palace *(below R)*. Compare with photo on page 27

Above, 50 year old bullet holes still riddle the railing in Saints Cyril and Methodius Orthodox Cathedral on Resslova Street. Below, the crypt as it appears today.

EPILOGUE

While no one will ever doubt for a moment the magnificent heroism of those brave men that parachuted into German-occupied Czechoslovakia, the debate will always rage about why they were sent at all. The act of sending them certainly resulted in far more Allied (and especially Czechoslovakian) deaths than German deaths. Important signs point to the British SOE as the culprit. Rather than see their pre-war Czechoslovakian spy ring disintegrate under German occupation they were willing to sacrifice any number of *Czechoslovakian lives* trying to retain some semblance of it.

Certainly the British SOE *was at least* as inept and theatrical as it was heroic. Their offices were located at 82 Baker Street in London, very near those of the fictional Sherlock Holmes. The organization was developed separately from British Military Intelligence by Prime Minister Winston Churchill to conduct sabotage, gather information and encourage revolt among German-occupied peoples of Europe. Churchill gave SOE the somewhat dramatic mission of "setting Europe ablaze".

From the start, military and professional critics in Britain called it "ungentlemanly, amateurish and underhanded". It certainly was amateurish in many respects. According to one very knowledgeable source (a former British officer) most of the staff of SOE had, "only the vaguest notion of what they should be doing, and precious little idea of how to go about it". He cited the following as an example:

> When he became information officer of SOEs *F Section* in 1941, Captain Maurice Buckmaster was told that the "general idea" was for him to gather information about occupied France. Seeking something more than a "general idea" he inquired about the mission of SOE and was told it was "subversive activities". Naturally, he asked the nature of the subversive activities. The answer he got from his superior was, "I'm not too clear myself, but I think the idea is to sabotage industrial facilities in France".

Another example will give an even better idea of the general ineptitude of SOE clandestine operations in Europe during World War II. An experienced German Abwehr agent, Major Hermann Giskes, uncovered the SOE plan for Holland in March 1942 and was able to capture **every** Dutch SOE agent sent from England through mid 1944! Of the 51 Dutch agents trained in England by SOE and sent to Holland during the period, the Germans executed 46. The other 5 were either "turned" to work for the Germans or imprisoned. The Germans had intercepted over 4000 "secret" SOE messages resulting in at least 350 additional arrests in Holland and Belgium. The following supplies were air dropped **not** into SOE agent hands, **but into** German hands in Holland: 34,000 pounds of explosives, 8000 pistols, 300 machine guns, 2000 hand grenades and over a half-million rounds of ammunition. The SOE also gave the Germans 75 radio transmitters, 40 bicycles and copious amounts of food and clothing during the period. Some German units did *less harm* to the Allied cause than SOE clandestine operations did.

The SOE probably would have continued to send him more agents and information until war's end if Major Giskes had not voluntarily ended his "sting" by sending the SOE a very sarcastic message on his 10 operational "Dutch" transmitters on April Fools Day of 1944.

During World War II a bust of Reinhard Heydrich was placed atop a German memorial on the spot where he was wounded at the corner of Kirchmeyerstraße and Klein Holeschowitzerstraße in the Praha suburb of Kobilisi. Quite naturally, that memorial was removed at the end of the war. For strange reasons no one has ever seen fit to erect any sort of memorial to Gabčík and Kubiš and the other heroes of the Czechoslovakian resistance on that spot. Perhaps such a memorial will be erected in the future.

APPENDIX A - GUIDE TO PRONUNCIATION FOR AMERICANS

Abwehrabteilung	= Ob-ware-ob-ty-lung
Eduard Beneš	= Ed-ward Ben-esh
Bohemia (CZ)	= Boh-he-me-a (see Böhmen)
Böhmen (G)	= BoAY-men (see Bohemia)
Brno	= Brr-no
Bulovka	= Boo-loaf-ka
Jaroslav Čvančara	= Yaro-slav Chvan-chara
Carpathian	= Car-pot-e-on
Černínsky	= Chair-nin-ski
Cholmondeley Park	= Chum-ley Park
Karel Čurda	= Car-el Chur-da
Deuxième Bureau	= Doo-ze-em Be-hRow
Elbe (G)	= El-ba (see Labe)
Karl Frank	= Karl Fronk
Josef Gabčík	= Yo-sef Gob-cheek
Viliam Gerik	= Vil-ee-om Gair-eek
Reinhard Heydrich	= Rine-heart High-dreesch
Hlavni	= Hlov-nee
Hlucin	= Hul-seen
Hradčany	= Hrod-chony
Jungfern-Breschen (G)	= Yung-fairn Bres-chen (see Panenské Břežany)
Eugen Krantz	= Oy-gen Kron-ts
Jan Kubiš	= Yon Ku-bish
Labe (CZ)	= Lob-eh (see Elbe)
Lidice	= Lee-dee-tseh
Mähren (G)	= May-ren (see Moravia)
Tomáš Masaryk	= Toe-mosh Masa-reek
Matyášuv Gate	= Mat-tee-ya-shoev Gate
Arnošt Mikš	= Ar-no-scht Meek-scht
Moravia (CZ)	= Moh-ra-vee-a (see Mähren)
Moldau (G)	= Mole-dow (see Vltava)
von Neurath	= fon Noy-rot
Odra (CZ)	= Oh-dra (see Oder)
Oder (G)	= Oh-der (see Odra)
Lina von Osten	= Lee-na fon O-sten
Panenské Břežany (CZ)	= Pon-en-skeh Bre-zhon-ee (see Jungfern-Breschen)
Praha (Prague, Prag)	= Pra-ha
Protektorate	= Pro-tek-tor-rot
Reichsprotektor	= Rikes-pro-tek-tor
Ruthenia	= Ru-ten-ee-a
Saints Cyril and Methodius	= Sear-ul and Meh-toad-ee-us
Sudeten	= Sue-date-en
Paul Thümmel	= Paul Tuee-mel
Ufer	= Oo-fer
Václavském náměstí	= Vah-klov-skem na-mess-tea
Josef Valčík	= Yo-sef Vall-cheek
Vltava (CZ)	= Vla-tah-vah (see Moldau)

Words followed by (CZ) are Czechoslovakian words which have a German (G) equivalent in this list.
Words followed by (G) are German words which have a Czechoslovakian (CZ) equivalent in this list.
Rs (and řs) are rolled in both spoken Czech and spoken German.

APPENDIX B - RECAP OF SOE PARACHUTE DROPS IN CZECHOSLOVAKIA 10-41 TO 5-42

OPERATION PERCENTAGE (04 October 1941) Corporal František Pavelka, arrested three weeks after arrival.

OPERATION ANTHROPOID (28/29 December 1941) was composed of Sergeants Josef Gabčík and Jan Kubiš and was parachuted into Czechoslovakian in a combined flight with *Operations Silver A* and *Silver B*. The assignment accepted by Gabčík and Kubiš prior to departure was to, "at the right time and in the right place and under ideal conditions, perform sabotage or terroristic activity important enough that it will become well known *even outside* of Czechoslovakia". Col František Moravec suggested to Gabčík that they try to kill either Acting Reichsprotektor Reinhard Heydrich or his Secretary of State Karl Frank.

OPERATION SILVER A (28/29 December 1941) consisting of Lieutenant Alfréd Bartoš, Sergeant Josef Valčík, and Corporal Jiří Potůček. *Valčík died in the church crypt on 18 June 1942, Bartoš died of gunshot wounds on 22 June and Potůček was shot and killed on 02 August 1942.*

OPERATION SILVER B (28/29 December 1941) consisting of Sergeants Vladimír Škacha and Jan Zemek, lost all their equipment and went underground.

OPERATION ZINC (27/28 March 1942) consisting of Lieutenant Oldřich Pechal, Sergeant Arnošt Mikš, and Corporal Viliam Gerik, dropped late and landed in Slovakia, barely escaping capture, losing all their equipment. Pechal was captured and eventually executed on 22 September 1942 at Mauthausen concentration camp. Mikš died helping BIOSCOP in the attempt to recover their equipment. Gerik was unable to find the underground, surrendered in Praha and was "turned" by the Gestapo. During a 1943 attempt to rejoin the resistance Gerik was arrested by the Gestapo and sent to Dachau concentration camp. *He was hung in Czechoslovakia as a German collaborator on 29 April 1947.*

OPERATION OUT DISTANCE (27/28 March 1942) consisting of Lieutenant Adolf Opálka, Corporal Ivan Kolařík and Sergeant Karel Čurda, landed badly. Opálka injured his leg, Kolařík lost all his papers and committed suicide rather than to be captured. Čurda made it to Praha. The Rebecca aircraft homing beacon they brought from England was plowed up next day by the farmer on who's land they had buried it. He turned it over to the Germans. *Adolf Opálka took part as a look-out in the attempt to kill Reinhard Heydrich and was subsequently killed in the shoot-out in the church. Čurda responded to the reward offered for Heydrich's assassins and was "turned" by the Germans. He was hung on 29 April 1947.*

The CANNONBURY RAID on the Škoda Works at Plzeň by the British Royal Air Force (RAF) on 26 April 1942 was supposed to interrupt production of war materiel. Despite good weather and locating fires set at great risk by Bartoš, Opálka, Gabčík, Kubiš and Valčík only one of the RAF bombers succeeded in finding the factory, and its bombs landed five miles away!

OPERATION BIOSCOP (27/28 April 1942) consisting of Sergeants Bohuslav Kouba, Josef Bublík, and Jan Hrubý, reached Praha safely. With the help of Mikš of OUT DISTANCE, Valčík of SILVER A and Ata Moravec of the safe-house family, Kouba returned to the airdrop zone to recover his equipment. In the ensuing ambush Mikš killed a policeman and himself, and Kouba committed suicide in his jail cell after being captured.

OPERATION BIVOUAC (27/28 April 1942) consisting of Sergeants František Pospíšil, Jindřich Čoupek, and Corporal Libor Zapletal. Čoupek and Zapletal fell into German hands within a few days and explained SOE training to the Gestapo before revealing their Czech contact addresses. Ten Czech civilians were executed as a result and Pospíšil was soon captured.

OPERATION STEEL (27/28 April 1942) Corporal Oldřich Dvořák, lost his radio transmitter and replacement crystals for SILVER A to the Germans and was shot and killed as he tried to flee to Slovakia.

OPERATION TIN (29/30 April 1942) consisting of Sergeants Jaroslav Švarc, and Ludvík Cupal, lost all equipment upon landing. Švarc suffered internal injuries which he survived, only to die in the church crypt in Praha on 18 June 1942. *Cupal committed suicide to avoid capture by the Gestapo on 15 January 1943.*

OPERATION INTRANSITIVE (29/30 April 1942) consisting of Lieutenant Václav Kindl, Sergeant Bohuslav Grabovský, and Corporal Vojtěch Lukaštík, lost all equipment upon landing. Kindl and Grabovský were captured. Kindl was shot and killed by accident after having been "turned" by the Germans. Grabovský was executed at Terezín. *Lukaštík was found by the Germans and killed in 1943.*

APPENDIX C - MISCELLANEOUS INFORMATION

As chief of the Sicherheitsdienst *(in Besoldungsgruppe B4)* or as ⚡-Obergruppenführer *(in Besoldungsgruppe C3)* Heydrich was paid 19,000 RM (about US$7600.00) per year at a time when a German army private made 1,410 RM (about US$565.00) per year.

The rate at which Czechoslovakian Crowns (K=Koruna) could be exchanged into US dollars in 1941 was about three and a half cents each.

The rate at which German Marks (RM= Reichsmarks) could be exchanged into US dollars in 1941 was about 40 cents each.

The Orthodox Cathedral of Saints Cyril and Methodius was called the St. Karl Boromeo Church by the Germans during World War II.

Reinhard and Lina Heydrich had three children: two sons, Klaus and Heider, and a daughter Silke. Lina Heydrich was pregnant with their fourth child when Heydrich was assassinated.

Soldiers of ⚡-Gebirgsjäger Regiments 6 and 11 of the 6th ⚡-Gebirgsjäger Division "Nord" were entitled to wear an embroidered honor title cuff band saying **Reinhard Heydrich** on the cuff of the left arm of their uniform tunic. The units were named for Heydrich after his death. An example of the Heydrich cuff band is reproduced at the top of the front cover of this book.

Reinhard Heydrich's widow Lina remarried after World War II and was known as Lina Heydrich-Maninnen. She was awarded a small pension as the widow of a German General killed in action and made a living operating a hotel on Fehmarn Island in the Baltic Sea.

Reinhard Heydrich's death is officially noted in the Death Register of the City of Praha, volume1/1942, entry 348.

The cover name assigned to Josef Gabčík for OPERATION ANTHROPOID was Zdenda. Jan Kubiš' cover name was Navratil.

The memorial tablet attached to the outside of the Orthodox Cathedral of Saints Cyril and Methodius on Resslova Street in Praha was created by František Belsky in 1947. It says:

In this temple of Saints Cyril and Methodius, these members of the national
underground died for our freedom on 18 June 1942
ADOLF OPÁLKA, JOSEF GABČÍK, JAN KUBIŠ,
JOSEF VALČÍK, JOSEF BUBLÍK, JAN HRUBÝ,
JAROSLAV ŠVARC, Pastors GORAZD, PETŘEK, SONNEVEND and other
Czech patriots who hid them or helped them in any way.
They will stay in our memory forever.

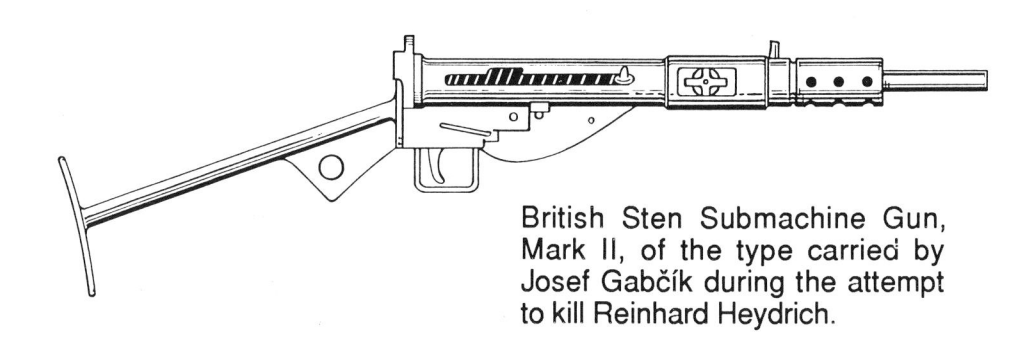

British Sten Submachine Gun, Mark II, of the type carried by Josef Gabčík during the attempt to kill Reinhard Heydrich.

BIBLIOGRAPHY

BOOKS:

Aronson, Shlomo: REINHARD HEYDRICH UND DIE FRUHGESCHICHTE VON GESTAPO UND SD, München, 1971.

Bradley, John: LIDICE, Ballantine Books, New York, 1972.

Burgess, Alan: SEVEN MEN AT DAYBREAK, Evans Brothers, London, 1960.

Calic*, Edouard: REINHARD HEYDRICH, William Morrow and Company, New York, 1985.

Čvančara, Jaroslav: AKCE ATENTÁT, Magnet Press, Praha, 1990.

Deschner, Günther: REINHARD HEYDRICH, Stein and Day, New York, 1981.

Farago, Ladislas: THE GAME OF THE FOXES, David McKay Co., New York, 1971.

GERMANY BASIC HANDBOOK, Ministry of Economic Warfare, London W.1., 1944.

Garber, G S: THE LIFE AND TIMES OF REINHARD HEYDRICH, David McKay Co., New York, 1980.

Heydrich, Lina: LEBEN MIT EINEM KRIEGSVERBRECHER, Paffenhofen, 1976.

Höhne, Heinz: DER ORDEN UNTER DEM TOTENKOPF, Verlag der Spiegel, Hamburg, 1966.

Ivanov, Miroslav: TARGET HEYDRICH, Hart-Davis, London, 1974.

Ivanov, Miroslav: DER HENKER VON PRAG, Edition q, Berlin 1993

Manvell, Roger: SS GESTAPO, Ballentine Books, New York, 1969.

Miller, Russell: THE RESISTANCE, Time-Life Books, Alexandria, VA, 1979.

Welles, Summer: AN INTELLIGENT AMERICAN'S GUIDE TO THE PEACE, Dryden Press, New York, 1945.

Wiener, Jan: THE ASSASSINATION OF HEYDRICH, Grossman, New York, 1969.

Wistrich, Robert: WHO'S WHO IN NAZI GERMANY, Bonanza Books, New York, 1982.

THE WORLD ALMANAC BOOK OF FACTS, World Telegram, New York, 1941.

Wykes, Alan: HEYDRICH, Ballatine Books, New York, 1972.

PERIODICALS:

After the Battle Quarterly #24, Battle of Britain Prints, London, 1979.

FILMS:

OPERATION DAYBREAK: 119 minutes, color (video), Warner Brothers, USA, 1975.

SS-3: 90 minutes, color (video), International Historical Films, Chicago, IL 60629-0035 USA, 1990

Highly recommended for its objectivity.

THE PRAHA PARACHUTIST WINGS

This beautiful set of miniature parachutist wings is finely struck in steel dies from pure copper. The Orthodox cross on the parachute is hand-filled with genuine cloisonne. The cloisonne is fired at 1400 degrees F to fuse it with the copper, and the entire piece is then artfully antiqued by hand. Two military grip pins make it easy and safe to attach to clothing.

A portion of the purchase price of each copy of this book, and of each set of PRAHA PARACHUTIST WINGS is donated to the Orthodox Cathedral of Saints Cyril and Methodius in Praha. Wear a set of wings with pride! **Cost is only US$5.00 each mailed anywhere in the world prepaid.**

Order from USM, Inc., PO Box 810, Lakeville MN, 55044-0810 USA

OTHER BOOKS PUBLISHED BY USM, INC. INCLUDE:

All-American Wonder, The Military Jeep 1941-1945, Volume I
All-American Wonder, The Military Jeep 1941-1945, Volume II
Capone's Chicago
Ford Military Vehicles 1941-1945, Master Parts List
Hitler's New German Reichschancellery in Berlin 1938-1945
Hitler - The Hoffmann Photos
Jeep Willys-Overland Model MB, Master Parts List, 1941-1945
Jeep Willys-Overland Model MB, Maintenance Manual, 1941-1945
Nazi Militaria - Fake or Real?
Nazi Paramilitary Organizations and Their Badges
World War II Envelope Art of Cecilé Cowdery

Order from your favorite bookseller. If not available, write USM, Inc., PO Box 810, Lakeville MN, 55044-0810 USA

If you would like to make a donation
to the preservation of the Orthodox Cathedral of Saints Cyril and Methodius in Praha you may mail it to:

Duchovní spávce
Orthodox Cathedral of Saints Cyril and Methodius
Resslova 9
CZ-120 00 Praha
CZECH REPUBLIC

OPERATION ANTHROPOID

Josef Bublík Duchovní Čikl Předseda Církevní Josef Gabčík Biskup Gorazd Jan Hrubý Jan Kubiš Adolf Opálka Dr Petřek Obce Sonnevend Jaroslav Švarc Josef Valčík